. . . .

Library and Archives Canada Cataloguing in Publication

Jongsma, Perry
    Reading between the wines : the story of a traveling book club / authors, Perry Jongsma, Pat Maaten, Kathleen Mundy ; editor, Fina Scroppo, art direction, Stephanie White ; photographers, Madison D'Andrea, Alyssa Jongsma.

ISBN 978-0-9864846-0-5

    1. Book clubs (Discussion groups)--Handbooks, manuals, etc. 2. Women travelers. 3. Entertaining. 4. Menus. I. Maaten, Pat II. Mundy, Kathleen III. Title.

LC6619.J65 2010   028'.8   C2009-907037-5

. . . .

First Edition

Editing by **Fina Scroppo**
Art Direction by **Stephanie White**
Photography by **Madison D'Andrea** and **Alyssa Jongsma**
Illustrations by **McMillanDigitalArt.com**
Published by **BGO Group Inc.**
Printed and bound in Canada by **Andora Graphics**

All inquiries should be addressed to **readingbetweenthewines.ca**

To Alex, Ken and Ron,
for your extraordinary
patience and support

reading between the wines

the story of a traveling book club

perry jongsma | pat maaten | kathleen mundy

contents

let us introduce ourselves

kathleen mundy | perry jongsma | pat maaten

IN 2001, we were a group of six women who innocently started a book club, completely unaware of the impact it would have on our own personal lives, much less the fodder it would eventually provide for writing this book. Within the first year, we started to refer to ourselves as The Giller Girls or *GGs* for short. We don't know exactly how this evolved, but it was loosely based on the Giller Prize and coincidently matched the short form for the Governor General's Award (The *GGs*), both of which are preeminent Canadian literary awards. We reasoned that this lent a somewhat academic credibility to our group, but in truth it was simply one of those names that sounded great and just stuck!

In the beginning, our goal for starting a book club was to have regular meetings with other women to discuss books, a forum to get us out of our daily routine. The occasion was an opportunity to take time for ourselves, to enjoy the company and conversations of others without the intrusion of work, family or outside responsibilities. We had only envisioned traveling through the pages of the books we read. But, over time, our book club became more than a club about books. Subsequent new friendships and the fun we had together prompted us to take our club to new heights and add travel to the mix. We wanted to experience new places and emotions, laugh till our sides hurt and our hearts lifted.

Now, the three of us want to share that experience and formula with you. *Reading Between the Wines: The Story of a Traveling Book Club* was inspired by the exploits of the *GGs*, from our monthly book club meetings to our ultimate annual getaways. We started what we thought would simply be a book club, but quickly discovered that we had created a nurturing, safe and sound environment where we could explore new horizons. It wasn't just about the books or the opinions of the books; it was the great time we experienced together.

And people have taken notice, wherever we go. We are continually amazed at the reaction we receive when we tell strangers we meet on our getaways about our club and how it came to be. Never was this more apparent than during our New York getaway, where we felt the collective appreciation for what we had created in our book club, further inspiring us to write this book – a sort of journal, guidebook and roadmap.

So what you have is our attempt to share with you, the reader, all the joys we've experienced with our beloved book club. We've come a long way since our first meeting. It's our hope that our book will give you the same inspiration to create your own book club journey with your own collection of adventures.

book | bok | noun

1. > a collection of paper,
   parchment or other material
   with text or pictures
   between two covers and
   bound together along one
   edge within covers
2. > the print that binds the *GGs*
   one night a month for as
   long as the wine lasts

This book is our story. It's the story of the Giller Girls, better known as the GGs. We started what we thought would be an ordinary book club, but our ordinary book club has evolved into so much more.

beginnings:
our book club story

In this chapter, you'll read the story of how we, the *GGs*, started our book club. From very humble beginnings and a questionable first book selection, we established the foundation for a lasting tradition – the *GG* Book Club.

first steps

first steps | How the founding members of the GG Book Club came together despite some unlikely circumstances.

Before we jump into how we formed and grew our book club, it's important for us to tell you what kind of book club we created. As you'll read in the pages that follow we're not your ordinary book club. Countless times we catch ourselves telling others how much we love our book club and reflecting on the fabulous times we've had together. Being in the company of our *GG* book club sisters inspires us, whether it's while discussing the latest book selection or participating in one of our infamous getaways. The connections that we've forged through our book club year after year are something that we really want to share with others. Although none of us is an author in her own right, what better way to share than by telling our story.

Our meetings breed creativity, but never competition, from the food served to the books selected. There's an unconditional acceptance of who you are. It's never about one-upmanship. It's a relaxed environment where you can be as enthusiastic as you want to be on just about any topic.

It's about one place (where we gather usually once a month) where you are never judged. And what happens at book club stays at book club. This book is a stimulant, to help other women get started on their own personal journey.

" It is not so much our friends' help that helps us, as the confidence of their help when in need." —*Epicurus (341-270 BC)*

› from the start

Our book club grew out of very humble beginnings and, in retrospect, it's amazing that it ever started at all. Truth be told, the genesis of the *GG* Book Club was in a hockey arena. For several years, three couples held season tickets for our local hockey team's games. It was a good excuse to get out of the house. It certainly wasn't the hockey that brought the women out on those cold winter nights, but rather the camaraderie of good friends getting together on a regular basis. The reluctance to disappoint each other kept the women coming back. While the men watched the game, the women, along with half-hearted attempts to follow the action on the ice, bonded.

As each season drew to a close, the women talked about finding something else besides our hockey tickets as our "excuse" for getting out of the house. One of us kept suggesting we start a book group, but the idea needed some help to come to life. When the group finally decided to let their season tickets lapse, the thought of missing what had come to be a special time together loomed ominously. This reality galvanized us into action, and gave us the motivation to form the Giller Girl Book Club, what has affectionately come to be referred to as the *GG* Book Club.

We knew other women who belonged to book clubs and wondered if their models might be something we should consider. We were three women with three different perspectives on what being in a book club entailed. We all agreed that we liked to read, but somehow we just never seemed to have the motivation to broaden our literary horizons or take the time to do it right. We were simply grateful when someone loaned us the latest popular book – something we could read without the effort of selecting a title or tracking it down in the maze of bookstore aisles.

› how do you start?

In the beginning, with no rules and no formal format or protocol to follow, we, the original three women, appointed ourselves founding members. Each of us invited a friend or neighbor to a meeting to test the idea of creating a book club. We just wanted to make sure that this concept would fly. The only constraint at the time was no family members, not because

GG members are...

> friends, friends of friends and neighbors
> voracious readers at all times of day or night
> casual readers squeezing in the book on weekends or late nights
> fun-loving women from a variety of interests – from athletic types to travelers to cooks (great ones, not-so-great ones and some even with kitchen phobias)

we didn't like our families, but because the point of this endeavor was to broaden our horizons and cultivate an opportunity for getting to know new people.

There was nothing formal about our initial gathering. It was just an agreement to discuss the possibility of forming a book club. As we contemplated who to invite, we didn't think it was important that everyone know each other ahead of time. What we did think was important was that each member be someone that one of us knew and respected and thought would be a great addition to the group. We were looking for women who loved to socialize. And if they liked to read books as well, then that was even better. It couldn't be simpler.

> Books, like friends, should be few and well chosen. Like friends, too, we should return to them again and again for, like true friends, they will never fail us – never cease to instruct." *– Charles Caleb Colton*

So, with a small group of six, we had our starting point. It sounded simple at first, but many of us were torn between having more commitments in our lives and a night out to call our own. We all loved the idea of adding a personal dimension to our doing-for-everybody-else lifestyles, but because we honored our precious little personal time, we were naturally guarded.

We were worried about spending too much of our personal time on reading, especially if the books turned out to be dull. And the potential for having to make vain attempts at stimulating conversation about those books made us wary. Yes, even Perry, who never passes up the opportunity for socializing (she's the party girl of the group), had her doubts at first. Pat, who has become known as the pragmatic corporate woman in the group, always saw the possibilities and lent her energy to moving us forward. We had the motivation to start a book club; all we needed was to devise a formula to make it happen.

who are the GGs?
....

› we are a grand assortment of friends who have known each other for a long time, and some who are meeting for the first time

› we are mothers

› we are wives, partners, sisters, aunts and daughters

› we are entrepreneurs, corporate executives, philanthropists and professionals

› we are travelers who have fun and who experience great escapades

"I was a little apprehensive about the idea of joining a book club. After many years of child-induced sleep deprivation, I stopped reading. I still remember the book on my night table unopened and never read— *Serum*. It was the last book my mother gave me before she passed away. To date, I have never read this book. Why, I am not sure. If I couldn't read for my mother, could I read for this group?" —*Perry*

first get-together of the GGs | Testing out the idea of a book club, but not your everyday kind of book club.

With a core group and a commitment to make this work now in place, we embarked on a journey with many firsts. Here are some of those initial forays into the world of book clubbing – from how we got started to how we selected our first book to how we reviewed future books.

› getting together

With no books in hand, no agenda and no formalities (except for the promise of a glass of wine and appetizers), our initial group of six got together for our first discussion. None of us had previous book club experience, so we arrived at this first informal get-together with great anticipation, ready to become a part of this new adventure. We answered our first question – who would be in our group.

Scheduling meetings sounds simple and, for many, a regular day (like the first Tuesday of every month) can work out just fine. But we were a small group to start and we wanted to make sure that, as often as possible, everyone could attend every meeting. We decided that we would schedule the next get-together at the end of each meeting, and make every effort to have a meeting once a month.

There were other basic questions on getting started that we needed to answer before we could successfully get off the ground. Would we have a structured meeting format to accompany book selections? We decided we would simply write our own rules, leaving ourselves free to adapt as we went along. We also discovered that all of us were open to reading anything. Great, we had flexibility.

This led to the next question. How would we go about selecting our books? We had to open another Pinot Grigio – there were so many decisions to make.

> creating structure

After lots of discussion it was unanimous: we all wanted to pursue creating our own unique book club. Besides, any reason to get out with a group of girls always gets a thumbs-up, and reading a book and discussing it seemed a small price to pay. Everyone was interested in getting together at least once a month, an interval that would give us enough time to complete the book before discussing it at the next meeting.

Where we got hung up was on what to read and how to select our books. We talked at length about these quandaries but met with no resolution. We had consulted with women belonging to other book clubs and found their formats either too rigid, with little flexibility; or too loose, with little hope of sustainability.

We didn't want a lengthy book-selection process, with titles being suggested and voted on, put on a list and set out for the year. That sounded too much like a school curriculum. That's not to say it isn't a process that can work for some, but we knew it wasn't going to be right for us. Still, we needed to decide how we would choose our books. Then, we had a breakthrough. Perry and Kathleen, another member who is always keen to take on new challenges, volunteered to select our first book, much to the shared relief of everyone else. Before the evening came to a close, we decided on our next host. Luckily, Kathleen volunteered her home for the next book club meeting.

We had had a fantastic time with these initial efforts, and accomplished a lot. We'd created some of our own rules, decided how and when to hold meetings, and agreed that serving appetizers and wine were a great way to start. We'd decided to discuss the length of our meetings and rotation of venue the next time we got together.

We were off to a great beginning. There was definitely something to this book club concept after all. We still needed to test the waters, but we had high hopes. The fact that not everyone knew each other, or at least not very well, gave us all the more reason to want to get together again. We were all looking forward to the next meeting and, most of all, to receiving our first book. Little did we realize what we had started that evening – a connection and bond that would grow beyond any of our expectations.

questions to get started

Who do you include in your book club?

How often should you meet?

How do you select your first book?

How long should the books be?

How do you run a meeting?

How long should a meeting last?

selecting

selecting the first book | Who knew it could be so difficult to choose the inaugural book for our new book club?

How hard could it be to select a good book? If you think it's easy, just walk into any bookstore today without a specific title or topic in mind and look around. The selection is overwhelming. Making that first choice turned out to be a bigger responsibility than the two volunteers had expected. In fact, they were paralyzed by the decision as they walked through the maze of aisles in the biggest bookstore they could find in town. What if no one liked their book choice? Perry and Kathleen resolved this mission, at least for this time, by appointing themselves to make the choice together. Clever thinking – based on safety in numbers, each girl could blame the other if the group found the read a real disappointment. In the end, after great anguish, they opted for a book by an award-winning author.

gg discovery

The process of selecting the first book is like naming your firstborn. If you've chosen a bad title, you'll be forced to live with it for a long time.

· · · · · · · · · ·

> revolving host

The only formality for meeting number two, besides presenting the first book, was agreeing upon a host and a day for the next meeting. Before the night was finished, the six of us had established the order of hosting and, to this day, have very rarely deviated from it (except for including later members in the rotation). We also agreed that we'd keep things simple when hosting – never too fancy or with an air of competition. We had already set the standard with our first two get-togethers' simple offerings of appetizers and wine, our beverage of choice. This would be all we needed to host a meeting.

> receiving our first book

We were all pumped for our first official book club meeting. Of course, we didn't have a book to discuss yet, so there wasn't a lot of pressure for Kathleen, our host, to set a standard. But we developed another guiding principle for our future meetings – Perry and Kathleen suggested that the host of each meeting purchase books for all the members, just as they had done for this meeting. From this point forward, the element of surprise would always be part of our meetings. Presenting the next book at the end of each meeting, as a sort of big girl's loot bag, was a brilliant idea!

It was almost time to reveal the first book. To maintain the suspense for as long as possible, the duo gift-wrapped the book and unveiled their selection to anxious members near the end of the meeting. The first tradition of our book club was born that night.

As we had with the first, we made some progress during our second meeting. We decided how we would select our books – the host of the meeting would always make the selection and purchase a copy for each member. It's up to the host to decide when and how she would present her book choice. We also decided on size – roughly 300 pages in length, just to make sure we had a shot at finishing the book before the next meeting.

We saved the discussion about developing a meeting format until the next get-together, when we would have at least read our first book.

P.S. If a member had already read the book, we decided that it simply meant she'd have no homework and could just look forward to having fun at the next meeting. Or she might enjoy reading the book a second time.

book wrappings
. . . .
We've developed very creative ways to wrap our books – just to maintain the suspense a little longer. It's not required, but when hosts have the time or inclination, it adds more fun to the night.

Here are a few samples:
> *Seabiscuit* in a racing form
> *The Glass Castle* in aluminum foil
> *Under the Tuscan Sun* in Italian language newspaper, parcel style with red string
> *Eat, Pray, Love* in paper secured with a string of colourful beads
> *Tender at the Bone* in tear sheets from a food magazine
> *The Hatbox Letters* in an old-fashioned hatbox, wrapped to mimic a letter complete with stamp

book review

first official book review | Starting our journey, one meeting at a time.

Over the next few weeks, every member read their first book diligently. But the excitement waned the deeper we got into the story. Imagine the great disappointment when both Perry and Kathleen came to the same, slow realization that they had chosen an incredibly painful, depressing novel. This first book hadn't quite lived up to their expectations of grandeur. Surely, they kept thinking, it must get better. Just one more chapter, one more. Now they worried – would anyone want to continue the book club after wading through this book?

It was unanimous; no one liked the first book. But it was a critical milestone for us. We learned that it wasn't so important why we didn't like a book, but that we had established an environment comfortable enough for us to voice an opinion and discuss a book's merits. Our group was developing an easy, relaxed tone. And this, we soon realized, is what would set us apart from other book clubs.

66 There are books of which the backs and covers are by far the best parts." —*Charles Dickens*

GG book club
10 commandments

1 | You are priority #1. This is your night.

2 | Fun is a must.

3 | LOL (laugh out loud) at each other and yourself.

4 | Digression is accepted and expected.

5 | Never refuse a compliment or be reluctant to offer one.

6 | What happens at *GG* Book Club stays at book club.

7 | Read between the wines.

8 | Where the boys aren't and never will be!

9 | Never apologize for your book selection.

10 | Completing the book is expected but not mandatory.

gg discovery

If you think choosing your book is lots of fun, think again! Some of the GGs have spent days searching for the perfect book. Sometimes it takes awhile to learn a lesson... it's not about the book, it's about the FUN!

These commandments – including the ninth, a product of our experience with the first book – have evolved over the years. All in all, this list reflects the spirit and intent of the *GG* Book Club.

› process complete

We were on our way. We completed all of the getting-started questions. Nothing has ever been cast in concrete, though, and through the years we've learned to be flexible. We've added additional members; we don't always meet once a month; sometimes, we break the 300-page book limit, if there is a truly worthy book selection that warrants the deviation. And there is never any real structure to our meetings; flexibility is always the key.

› evolution of the GG Book Club

We fell into a rhythm of monthly book club meetings. Just the same, we never keep to a rigid schedule. Because many of our *GGs* travel, it's not always possible to have everyone available on a preset night. When it comes time to pick the next meeting date, it's typical to find all of us pulling out our day planners or smartphones, or even pocket-size calendars or scraps of paper. The host typically follows up with an e-mail to ensure that no one has forgotten about the next meeting date.

How long do our meetings last? There are *GGs* among us who might suggest that a meeting lasts until there's no wine left! But there are no set rules on how long a meeting should go. It all depends on the conversation, the general mood and what we have planned the next day.

We always make an effort at every meeting to have a lively discussion about the most recent book we've read. Sometimes there are reader questions at the back of the selected book and this helps to get conversation started. There are also many websites that offer book club-type questions. See sample websites in Chapter 9, "Book Club Blueprint." Sometimes, the person who has selected the book will bring questions to the next meeting, but more often than not, we can always count on one *GG* to arrive with a list of questions in hand.

meeting at a glance

> The host provides everything for the evening.

> A welcome bevie is provided upon arrival.

> Catch-up chat about any topic is encouraged until everyone arrives.

> Bites and bevies are served in any format.

> Book discussion often includes questions from other members and is led by the book's selector (last month's host).

> Digressions usually occur based on the interest (or lack thereof) in the book being discussed.

> A date is selected for the next meeting.

> A request for perhaps "just one more" digression, conversation, laugh or bevie is anticipated.

> Lots of socializing, chatter and laughter are encouraged.

> The next book is presented at the end of the evening.

> Responsible driving arrangements are made.

> Goodbyes are reluctantly exchanged.

"An ounce of prevention is worth a pound of cure. Place a large glass of water and two Advils on the nightstand before leaving the house for a book club meeting." —Perry

on the bookshelf

Who doesn't love a list! We've compiled a list of books from our first 60 *GG* Book Club meetings. In this chapter, we're giving you a candid review of how well we think these books have stacked up.

booklist

GG book list | The books we've read, along with our personal ranking system.

We've created a ranking system for the first 60 books we've read. Our picks cover the gamut of topics, from historical fiction to the latest bestseller, to please all preferences. While you never know what kind of book you're going home with, there's one thing you can count on: It'll be a surprise and, more often than not, a book choice you might not have made if left to your own devices.

These books are listed in the order that we read them. As you can see, there's no pattern to the genre or type of books we've read. It's simply up to the host's preference. See if you agree with our rankings.

GG review and ranking system

Ranking	What we said	What we really meant to say
♟♟♟♟♟	"Loved it, wanted more, can't wait for the movie"	Simply couldn't put the book down. Pure joy. Stayed up until the middle of the night to finish it. It was laced with emotion, filled with suspense
♟♟♟♟	"Thoroughly enjoyable. Perfect for book clubs"	Enjoyed reading the book from beginning to end. Had a positive reaction to the book
♟♟♟	"Good read, satisfying"	It was a light, easy read; but it wasn't a wow
♟♟	"Thought there was potential, constantly waiting for improvement"	Because it received great reviews or it was written by a familiar author, there were great expectations. But the book simply didn't deliver
♟	"Couldn't finish, or finished because I felt I had to"	It was an overwhelming disappointment

1 | *Anil's Ghost*
Michael Ondaatje

2 | *The Underpainter*
Jane Urquhart

3 | *Blackberry Wine*
Joanne Harris

• although it received great reviews and awards we found this painfully slow and disappointing

• this book inspired many emotions and thought-provoking dialogue; a satisfying read

• although a wine bottle might be a quirky central character this creative element provided charm

4 | *Divine Secrets of the Ya-Ya Sisterhood*
Rebecca Wells

5 | *A Student of Weather*
Elizabeth Hay

6 | *House of Sand and Fog*
Andre Dubus III

• the kindred sisterhood emotions we felt motivated us all to see the movie after reading the book

• this prairie town story hit close to home for a member and inspired conversation about our roots

• a painful clash of lives/cultures causes a downward spiral of emotions and leaves the reader feeling helplessly empathetic

" A great book should leave you with many experiences and slightly exhausted at the end. You should live several lives while reading it." —*William Styron*

7 | *Harry Potter and the
Philosopher's Stone*
J.K. Rowling

• it met with mixed
reviews; some
continued to read
the entire series,
while others
declined the fantasy

8 | *The Bonesetter's
Daughter*
Amy Tan

• we loved the
window to other
cultures and times.
A rich sample of the
conflict traditions
can inspire

9 | *Back When We
Were Grownups*
Anne Tyler

• a wonderful easy
read, requiring little
from the reader

10 | *The Red Tent*
Anita Diamant

• a glimpse into
another time. The
story of women
nurturing each other
and forming recurring
connections inspired
lengthy debate

11 | *Sheltering Rain*
Jojo Moyes

• a moderately
entertaining,
easy read

12 | *Seabiscuit*
Laura Hillenbrand

• one *GG* gained
insight into the
life of her jockey
grandfather. It was
a great ride

13 | *Too Close
to the Falls*
Catherine Gildiner

• the vivid
recollection of
childhood memories,
could have been the
personal experience
of any one of us

14 | *Crow Lake*
Mary Lawson

• a pleasurable read.
The story came
to life through the
complex character
development

15 | *Atonement*
Ian McEwan

• a well-written,
heart-wrenching
story of betrayal,
personal struggle
and tragedy between
siblings in pre-war
England

16 | *Without Reservations*
Alice Steinbach

• the central
character's
independence
inspired Pat and
Perry to visit the
locales in Paris
months later

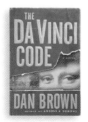

17 | *The Da Vinci Code*
Dan Brown

• a fantastically
informative mystery,
generating dialogue
and religious debate.
We were captivated
by the story; a true
page turner

18 | *The Lovely Bones*
Alice Sebold

• it was uniquely told
in a compassionate
manner; thought-
provoking with an
unexpected central
character

19 | *Confessions of a Shopaholic*
Sophie Kinsella

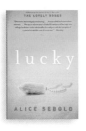

20 | *Lucky*
Alice Sebold

21 | *Where the Heart Is*
Billie Letts

• an unabashed homage to the consumer in all of us; a light summer read, perfect beach book

• a shocking read, essentially a memoir from the author's own experience, helped to understand the motivation for *The Lovely Bones*

• we were pleasantly surprised, this is a heart-warming story filled with everyday situations and human emotions

22 | *Under The Tuscan Sun*
Frances Mayes

23 | *A Good House*
Bonnie Burnard

24 | *Clara Callan*
Richard B. Wright

• this could be anyone's fantasy, a perfect what-if scenario to leave your life behind and start something totally new

• somewhat disappointing; a very ordinary and boring family made this a very slow read

• although the style of writing through letters was interesting at first, it became tedious by the end

25 | *The Last Crossing*
Guy Vanderhaeghe

• we were let down by the story based on previous novels by this author; painfully long and no emotional connection to the characters

26 | *The Amateur Marriage*
Anne Tyler

• the main character in the story was chronically unhappy and experienced unending conflicts in her relationship

27 | *The Romantic*
Barbara Gowdy

• a bit disappointing; the plot continually jumps forward and backward so often that it becomes tiresome

28 | *The Pelee Project*
Jane Christmas

• although not as inspiring as anticipated, Pelee Island became the destination of our book club's third travel getaway

29 | *Reading Lolita in Tehran*
Azar Nafisi

• it provided a window into the complex world of Muslim women; we had empathy for a culture under such censorship

30 | *Lolita*
Vladimir Nabokov

• a classic that was interesting to read, but also disturbing; this was a great follow-up to the previous read

31 | *The Five People You Meet in Heaven*
Mitch Albom

32 | *The Curious Incident of the Dog in the Night-time*
Mark Haddon

33 | *Nights of Rain and Stars*
Maeve Binchy

• the premise of the book is an interesting concept, with mortality being the central theme

• it is creatively written, giving us insight into the personal lives of people with Asperger's Syndrome

• a disappointing read because Binchy has long been one of our favorite authors. This book just seemed too predictable

34 | *Tender at the Bone*
Ruth Reichl

35 | *The Devil Wears Prada*
Lauren Weisberger

36 | *The Hot Flash Club*
Nancy Thayer

• it is emotional, very personal, incredibly real for anyone who has worked in the restaurant business; witty and funny

• we were unable to relate to the mean, sarcastic tone of the writing

• although for the most part this had a condescending tone, there were some humorous passages

37 | *The Good Earth*
Pearl S. Buck

• a fabulous, timeless story of the life and struggles of a poor Chinese family in the 1900s; the message could apply to any family today

38 | *A Complicated Kindness*
Miriam Toews

• an insightful view into the angst of a 16-year-old girl growing up in a Mennonite community

39 | *The Hatbox Letters*
Beth Powning

• a moving story of a recently widowed woman discovering her roots from her grandparents' letters

40 | *The Tiger Claw*
Shauna Singh Baldwin

• we had empathy for the suffering of the central characters as they searched to find each other in a war-torn Europe

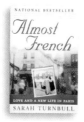

41 | *Almost French*
Sarah Turnbull

• a light-hearted read; who doesn't fantasize about life in Paris. Think of the romance, cafés and the shoes!

42 | *A Million Little Pieces*
James Frey

• at the time, we felt it unbelievable that someone could have lived and survived this life. The reality was he didn't

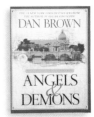

43 | *Love Storm*
Susan Johnson

44 | *Mao's Last Dancer*
Li Cunxin

45 | *Angels & Demons*
Dan Brown

• there are no words to explain our first venture into romantic pulp fiction

• a heart-wrenching true story of a boy growing up in a Chinese ballet school and later gaining asylum in the States in the '70s

• an exciting chase through famous landmarks in Rome to solve another complex mystery; loved the illustrated version

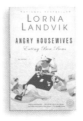

46 | *The Time In Between*
David Bergen

47 | *Angry Housewives*
Eating Bon Bons
Lorna Landvik

48 | *Suite Française*
Irène Némirovsky

• a connection of generations across the world in Vietnam, to a different time and place; sad and poignant

• the connections described among the women are similar to the bonds shared by the GGs

• an amazing true story of a woman's incredible strength of character trying to survive the Second World War

49 | Giller night for the GGs

We held a book club meeting on the actual night that the Giller Prize was being awarded. The Giller Prize is a Canadian book award that provided the genesis for our Giller Girl name. The clever *GG* hosting this night broke away from the tradition of purchasing the same book for each member. Instead, she 'served' all the books that were candidates for the Giller Prize, which were gift wrapped and organized on the table as part of her centerpiece. When it was time to receive our book, everyone was asked to select one of the packages randomly. It was the first and only time that we haven't taken home the same book. It was a little awkward discussing different books at the next book club, but it gave us the perfect opportunity to enjoy all five as we circulated the books among the group.

De Niro's Game
Rawi Hage

Bloodletting & Miraculous Cures*
Vincent Lam

The Perfect Circle
Pascale Quiviger

The Immaculate Conception
Gaétan Soucy

Home Schooling
Carol Windley

These books are not ranked since some were only read by one *GG*.

* *The winner that night*

50 | *The Thirteenth Tale*
Diane Setterfield

• the quintessential whodunit with captivating characters, unusual circumstances and an unpredictable ending

51 | *Never Let Me Go*
Kazuo Ishiguro

• this unusual story was not what was expected; kept waiting for it to improve

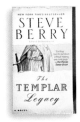

52 | *The Templar Legacy*
Steve Berry

• a complex historically based story; evoked lots of lively discussion

53 | *On Beauty*
Zadie Smith

• we didn't feel that it lived up to the glowing reviews; a tale of life, love, the hopes and unfulfilled dreams of two families

54 | *The Good Husband of Zebra Drive*
Alexander McCall Smith

• a lovely story of the simple day-to-day life of ordinary people living ordinary lives filled with compassion and humor

55 | *A Thousand Splendid Suns*
Khaled Hosseini

• a tragic, powerful novel bringing insight into the tortured life of an Afghan woman; poignantly moving

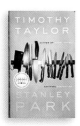

56 | *Stanley Park*
Timothy Taylor

• quirky characters provided insight into the behind-the-scenes complexity of the restaurant business: loved the Vancouver location

57 | *The Glass Castle*
Jeannette Walls

• we loved, loved, loved it; can't wait for the movie; tragically sad; how could a mother so selfishly destroy her entire family?

58 | *Eat, Pray, Love*
Elizabeth Gilbert

• an intriguing memoir chronicling a woman's journey of self-discovery

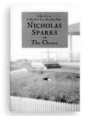

59 | *Loving Frank*
Nancy Horan

• a slow start developed into a dramatic and tragic ending for all characters; interesting insight into Wright's life

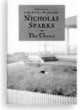

60 | *The Choice*
Nicholas Sparks

• after author's previous great successes, we found this one lacking originality

" So many books, so little time." —*Sara Nelson*

› from books to movies

Not surprisingly, many of the books we've read have been made into big-name movies. Sometimes, we've been pleasantly surprised with how a movie could be so true to a book; other times, we felt it might have been better simply to leave a good book alone.

Here's our take on the success of turning the books we've read into big-screen movies.

	Preferred the book	Preferred the movie	Liked them both
Divine Secrets of the Ya-Ya Sisterhood			✔
House of Sand and Fog			✔
Seabiscuit			✔
Atonement		✔	
The Da Vinci Code	✔		
Where the Heart Is			✔
Under the Tuscan Sun	✔		
Lolita	✔		
The Devil Wears Prada		✔	
Angels & Demons			✔

Seabiscuit

Laura Hillenbrand

Bevie match-ups: Wines from California (such as Pinot Noir or Chardonnay).

Why the book was chosen: One of our *GG*s is a racehorse owner, and has a particular affinity for horses. So it was no surprise that she selected this particular book.

Our impression: Hillenbrand invites us into the world of horse racing, with its joyous victories and heart-wrenching disappointments. We follow the changing lives of the jockey, trainer and owner on Seabiscuit's journey from precocious colt to famous, much-loved and wildly successful racehorse. The path to victory was not an easy one for Seabiscuit, who captured the hearts of many Americans yearning for a hero as an escape from the Depression in the 1930s. The book was a wonderful read; Hillenbrand gives us an exhilarating ride. A winner, right out of the gate.

Theme: An assortment of horse sculptures decorated the family room and our books were wrapped in a racing form from the local racetrack.

> GG question from the night: How does the life of a jockey from this era compare to that of the sports heroes of today?

Personal connection or meeting highlight: Our shortest (in stature only) *GG* was shocked to learn about the details of the life her great-grandfather must have led as a professional jockey.

Crow Lake

Mary Lawson

Bevie match-ups: Wines from the Niagara Peninsula, Canada (such as Baco Noir or Gewürztraminer).

Why the book was chosen: One of our *GGs* read an article in the local newspaper about the fact that this author originally hailed from our hometown of Sarnia.

Our impression: Although the setting is written as northern Ontario, the story is based in our local area, which made the book choice all the more compelling for us. It's a story of a family bound together by the tragic loss of the parents. Two older brothers struggle to raise their two younger sisters and keep their family together.

As mothers, we felt compassion for the children. The carefully crafted development of the characters kept all of us engaged until the unexpected ending.

Theme: For ideas, see Casual Cottage in Chapter 6, "Themed Nights."

> **GG question from the night:** If the children were separated after the loss of their parents, how might their lives have been different?

Personal connection or meeting highlight: The author is actually from our area and when she came to give a reading at the local library, we made it a *GG* outing.

Atonement

Ian McEwan

Bevie match-ups: Wines from France (such as Burgundy or Riesling).

Why the book was chosen: With some of our members hailing from the United Kingdom, this seemed a perfect catalyst for sharing and learning more about each other.

Our impression: Set in pre- and post-war England, the book launches with a 13-year-old aspiring writer misinterpreting an encounter she witnesses her sister having with the housekeeper's son. This sets in motion a series of misunderstandings with life-changing repercussions for all involved.

The story explores class conflict, war, love, jealousy, innocence and guilt, all woven through a time of both peace and war. As much as we all loved the book, we were amazed at how much more we enjoyed the movie.

Theme: A simple spread of cheese, dried fruit and crackers, with a hearty pot of Welsh rarebit ready for dipping, set atop a grandmother's embroidered tablecloth. See recipe in Chapter 7, "*GG* Bites."

> **> *GG* question from the night:** Is it always possible to forgive someone who has betrayed you?

Personal connection or meeting highlight: The conversation of a war-torn Europe prompted discussion of traveling as a group. For more details, see Chapter 4, "Beginnings: Our Travel Story."

Without Reservations

Alice Steinbach

Bevie match-ups: *GG* Booktini: A classic martini as Alice enjoyed at the Bar Hemingway at the Ritz in Paris. Chianti wine to follow.

Why the book was chosen: One of the inaugural planners chose this book to reflect the joy and adventure of travel. A must read before our first *GG* getaway travel experience.

Our impression: This is a beautifully written story of a woman's travels through Europe. It's also a memoir of the author's self-discovery, with reflections

on her life – past, present and future – set against the backdrop of beautiful European cities. This book challenged all of us to consider whether we could leave our comfort zone to experience an entirely different lifestyle on a different continent.

Theme: The books were wrapped in maps of Italy, France and England. Assorted Italian and French cheeses and olives were served. For more ideas, see Tuscany at Home in Chapter 6, "Themed Nights."

> **GG question from the night:** Could you leave your life behind and move away on your own for one year?

Personal connection or meeting highlight: Later that year, Pat and Perry visited a number of Alice's favorite spots in Paris, and enjoyed the same sights, cafés and hotels that she discovered. They created a small photo album for all of the GGs with the highlights of their "Alice journey."

The Da Vinci Code

Dan Brown

Bevie match-ups: Wines from Umbria (such as Orvietio or Lungarotti).

Why the book was chosen:
The *GG*s have always been interested in travel and intrigue, so this book was chosen to widen our sense of adventure and motivate our spirit of exploration.

Our impression: We were all inspired and fascinated by this powerful and magnificent story of speculation about the holy grail, and Mary Magdalene's role in the history of Christianity. The book gave us an opportunity to learn more about and debate the controversy that surrounds the story of Christianity within these pages. Our group delighted in unraveling the secrets and surprises within the book that led to an unexpected twist at the end, assuring it a place on our Top 13 list.

> **GG question from the night:** Who would you pick to play Robert Langdon, the lead character? (And several guesses later, no one picked Tom Hanks!)

Personal connection or meeting highlight: The author mixed traceable truths and facts with historical landmarks, some of which had been visited by some of the *GG*s on their previous travels, providing an even more personal connection for our group.

The Lovely Bones

Alice Sebold

Bevie match-ups: A variety of favorite wines.

Why the book was chosen: Admittedly, teenage rape is a heavy subject, but the host felt the group was ready to tackle more challenging topics.

Our impression: This story is set in heaven and told through the voice of a 14-year-old girl who has been raped and murdered. In spite of what seems like an incredulous premise, the story is both haunting and hopeful. Early into the book, all of the *GGs* were skeptical about the subject matter, but by the end, they unanimously ranked it high for its merit and quality. In fact, we enjoyed the book so much that we read Alice Sebold's first book, *Lucky*, several book club meetings later.

> **GG question from the night:** Have you ever felt as though someone was trying to communicate with you from the 'in between'?

Personal connection or meeting highlight: This book was presented while we embarked on our first travel getaway. We circulated and signed each other's copy with a personal note that highlighted what the getaway meant to each of us. This made it an even more special keepsake.

The Good Earth

Pearl S. Buck

Bevie match-ups: Wines from the region of your choice (try Riesling or Beaujolais, both pair well with Asian food).

Why the book was chosen: This book made an impression on the host when she first read it in high school. When she saw that it was on Oprah's Book Club list, she wanted to share it with the group hoping they would love it as much as she had.

Our impression: A simple tale of a farmer family's life set in China in the 1930s. It's the story of a family's hopes, dreams, failures and disappointments as they endure civil war and learn to adapt in an ever-changing world. We felt *The Good Earth* poignantly touches on the timeless, universal themes of life: the importance of family, women's rights, class struggles, hardships, traditions and moral dilemmas.

Theme: The book was wrapped in brown paper and tied with red string and a Chinese coin. For more ideas, see **Asian Delight in Chapter 6, "Themed Nights."**

> **GG question from the night:** Did main characters Wang Lung and his wife O-lan ever really love each other?

Personal connection or meeting highlight: This book was given at the meeting that was also a surprise baby shower for one of our *GG*s. Appropriately, it exemplified what we were celebrating – the start of yet another cycle of life.

Mao's Last Dancer

Li Cunxin

9

Bevie match-ups: Wines from the region of your choice (select Gewürztraminer or Pinot Noir).

Why the book was chosen: A book review in the newspaper captivated our host.

Our impression: This is an inspirational memoir of a boy born into abject poverty in rural China. Through fate, hard work and dedication, he becomes an internationally renowned ballet dancer. Li poignantly expresses the heartache and loneliness of a six-year-old child training to be a dancer in a city distant from his family. We also learn about his struggle for success when he moves to the United States and finds himself between two very different worlds.

Theme: The books were wrapped in paper with Chinese symbols. Chopsticks were the cutlery of choice (even though we struggled) for an Asian-inspired dinner. For more ideas, see Asian Delight in Chapter 6, "Themed Nights."

> *GG* **question from the night:** What life do you think Li would have had if his parents had not agreed to send him to ballet school?

Personal connection or meeting highlight: Everyone was spellbound and amazed at this incredible true story. We enjoyed a lengthy, detailed discussion of the way the author himself lived a life of paradox – caught between communist-led poverty and the prosperity of the Western world.

Suite Française

Irène Némirovsky

Bevie match-ups: Wines from France (such as Red Bordeaux or Chablis).

Why the book was chosen: The sheer improbability of this book ever being published was reason enough for our host to select it.

Our Impression: The story is set and written during the German occupation of France in the Second World War. The author began this novel after fleeing Paris with her family to evade the Nazis. While living in a small town outside the city, the author is arrested and later dies in Auschwitz.

Her young daughters survive the war. The only memento they have of their mother are papers that they believe to be her journal. After the war, they couldn't bring themselves to read it because it was too painful. Decades later, in an effort to preserve their mother's words, the daughters typed out her perceived journal and discovered that it was actually two parts of a planned five-part novel.

> **GG question from the night:** Would you be able to put politics aside and see good in people in the same way some characters did in this novel?

Personal connection or meeting highlight: While we were all moved by the tragedies depicted in the book, we were equally intrigued by the circumstances surrounding its publication.

The Thirteenth Tale

Diane Setterfield

Bevie match-ups: Wines enjoyed by the British (such as Rioja or cream sherry).

Why the book was chosen: Everybody loves a whodunnit – it's the perfect companion with a cup of tea on a winter's night by the fire.

Our impression: Was it the English windswept moors, bleak houses and strange dysfunctional families that made this book a page-turner? Or was it just the author's masterful treatment of an old-fashioned Gothic tale of secrets, ghosts, sexual obsession, murder and madness? For our group, it was both. This book held our interest from the beginning, thanks to the main character, Vida Winter, who was portrayed as the most famous novelist of England. A story of twins held together by obligation, this tale unfolded to reveal more than anyone could have imagined. It's one of those perfect reads that reminded us of the stories of the Brontë sisters and Agatha Christie that we had read in our youth.

Theme: This was our Christmas meeting, with the table glistening from candlelight. An heirloom lace tablecloth, pristinely polished silver and several dainty nosegays festooned the table.

> **GG question from the night:** Both being twins, how much do Margaret and Miss Winters have in common?

Personal connection or meeting highlight: This was the night we selected our Secret Agents for our fifth *GG* travel getaway.

Stanley Park

Timothy Taylor

Bevie match-ups: Wines from the Okanagan Valley in British Columbia (such as Merlot or Pinot Blanc).

Why the book was chosen: This was our first book after our getaway to Vancouver. Who couldn't resist a book with the same title as the park we rode our bikes through?

Our impression: Stanley Park is the setting for this complex fictional story that combines the suspense of a crime that occurred decades ago with the current-day life of a struggling restaurant owner-chef, Jeremy. It provides a unique and quirky perspective of life in the restaurant business.

We could envision the locations described in the book, having ridden our bikes through Stanley Park on our getaway to Vancouver. For anyone who has ever worked in a restaurant, including one of our *GG*s, this book would add a new dimension of drama.

Theme: The books were wrapped in a map of Stanley Park that we should have used during our infamous bike ride in Stanley Park.

> **GG question from the night:** After reading the book, do you think differently of Stanley Park?

Personal connection or meeting highlight: The book brought back wonderful memories of our biking adventure through Stanley Park.

The Glass Castle

Jeannette Walls

13

Bevie match-ups: It was a simple offering – red or white table wine.

Why the book was chosen: The book seemed intriguing to the host. She believed the circumstances that provided the framework for the story seemed incredulous. She read it ahead of time just to be sure it didn't disappoint.

Our impression: Our group had mixed reactions to this book. Some could identify with the family dynamics, while others simply found it unfathomable. The account of such a dysfunctional family, although told with kindness and humor, was tragic. It was a fascinating tale of survival that depicted how a mother's artistic and eclectic vision of life along with a father's drinking problem left the author and her siblings often taking care of themselves.

Theme: The books were wrapped in aluminum foil and placed on the table with a plethora of candles and glass paperweights. The sparkling reflections were very fitting.

> **GG question from the night:** How did the absence of parental involvement hinder/help the children's development?

Personal connection or meeting highlight: Some of the GGs had experienced similar situations in their own lives (on a much smaller scale). The fact that they were comfortable enough to share them with the group speaks volumes about our club's supportive and comfortable environment.

> "You know you've read a good book when you turn the last page and feel a little as if you have lost a friend." —*Paul Sweeney*

best gg get-togethers

We call any opportunity to get together, with or without books, a *GG*-worthy event. Here are just a few of our favorite get-togethers.

"A" retro Christmas | A multi-generational evening with new traditions added to the *GG* format.

Christmas, 'tis the season of fun and entertainment. One of the *GG* Book Club's strengths is its format. From the start, it has provided a base upon which we've built layers of new ideas. And our time together at our retro Christmas night, was no exception.

What made this night unique was that we staged ourselves instead of staging the table or the room. We turned back the clock, and revisited a time and place that would make any girl smile. We set the mood with some great tunes and relived the 1950s through to the '80s.

The idea and inspiration for the night originated from four books that we had read over the past couple of years. *The Divine Secrets of the Ya-Ya Sisterhood* by Rebecca Wells, *Angry Housewives Eating Bon Bons* by Lorna Landvik, *The Hot Flash Club* by Nancy Thayer and *Tender at the Bone* by Ruth Reichl reminded us about the importance of mothers and the influence our own moms still have on us today. So, as a tribute to our moms, we celebrated their memory by using recipes we remember fondly from our childhood.

› pre-party

Now that we had a theme for our Christmas gathering, we needed to source a retro wardrobe to reflect the time frame. There is no end to the creative genius of the *GG*s. One of us, a true fashionista, has a wardrobe that we all lust over. She has timeless pieces from years of collecting, in addition to some great finds that aren't so classic. In honor of our retro theme, our fashionista graciously opened her closet and offered to loan out some of her most spectacular pieces.

So, on a Sunday afternoon before the December book club meeting, we found ourselves trying on different outfits that had been in vogue over the years. Laughter filled the air as we tucked in shoulder pads that would humble a quarterback, traded colorful Pucci print caftans and tossed around velvet embellished jackets. We were ready to embrace the eras gone by. We took our perfectly coordinated outfits home until we were ready to don them for our retro Christmas celebration.

> party night

Coincidentally, this Christmas meeting was at the home of our fashionista. On that evening, our host greeted us at the door wearing a classic silk dress, true to the Jackie O style, and long gloves that accentuated the timeless look. The remaining *GG*s arrived sporting glittering gowns, shoulder pads, polyester pantsuits – a truly eclectic collection. Some of the girls even went so far as to emphasize their look with retro hairstyles à la Farrah Fawcett and Jaclyn Smith of *Charlie's Angels*. We really were a sight to behold.

Each *GG* brought a retro appetizer – a personal favorite (see menu) over the years from her mother's kitchen. The evening quickly became a family affair as Perry's son, who had just returned for Christmas break from university on the East Coast, surprised us by serving Christmas booktinis, resplendent in a waiter's attire. We also designated a *GG*'s daughter as photographer to commemorate the evening. It was a time to just kick up our heels, enjoy our company, with or without a book. The special night became a multigenerational event, filled with memories of our mothers, retro regalia and friendship. The picture was complete. A toast to our mothers!

"A" Retro
Christmas Menu
•
our mom's appetizers
pineapple meatballs
shrimp dip
layer cake with drunken fruit
shortbread
•
welcome bevie
chocolate raspberry booktini

For recipes, see Chapter 7, "GG Bites," and Chapter 8, "GG Bevies"

"A" Christmas gifts

. . . .

monogrammed
apple basket

amber earrings

amaryllis

angel

Australian aboriginal
art

Ancore – Il Divo CD

angel pottery
centerpiece

appetizer bowl

> new traditions begin

We began another tradition at this Christmas meeting – it has become the occasion for our annual selection of the following year's travel planners. You'll understand the importance of this assignment as you read **Section 2, Bon Voyage**. Our getaway planners need lots of time to plan a covert operation that includes transportation, restaurant and hotel bookings, none of which is revealed until hours or minutes before the adventure. Because there are so many details to sort through, we decided to partner the task. On this evening, the two *GGs* who were lucky enough to receive a book with the word "planner" written on the gift tag from the stack of elaborately gift-wrapped books become the designated planners. **See Chapter 5, "GG Getaways,"** for more inspiration and stories about our getaways. While it's rare that we discuss a book on a night like this, we make a valiant effort. This is our evening to celebrate our great friendships and reminisce about great times over the year.

As if there hadn't been enough excitement already, we added another ritual that night – the exchange of Christmas gifts. But in typical *GG* fashion this wasn't your conventional gift exchange.

On this night, everyone's gift had to start with the letter A, with an intent to work our way through the entire alphabet. This speaks to our commitment to book club. We placed the elaborately wrapped gifts on the coffee table, and the ceremony of their selection began.

Here's how the selecting game works: Taking turns based on a drawing of numbers, the *GG* with #1 selects any gift from the pile. No gifts are unwrapped until the end.

Each successive *GG*, one by one, can either:

❶ "steal" an already selected gift (if there's one they really like) or

❷ be adventurous and go for a gift that still hasn't been plucked from the pile.

If a *GG* chooses to steal, the person whose gift is stolen now repeats her turn and either:

❶ steals another person's gift (she cannot immediately steal back the gift that was just stolen from her) or

❷ selects a new gift.

More often than not, we *GGs* are drawn to the wrappings. This causes tissue-flying and ribbon-unfurling gift theft and envy among friends. Too much fun!

> off-site activities

On this same evening, our husbands took advantage of a unique opportunity. They gathered for dinner at Pat's home, where they enjoyed a feast of East Coast lobsters personally delivered by Perry's son (remember our personal bartender?) that had arrived that day. When we're away on our travel getaways, our *GGBs* (Giller Girl Boys, an endearing moniker for all *GG* spouses) will generally get together one night for dinner. That they did, too, on this Christmastime occasion, made it a truly special evening for everyone.

❝ Laugh and the world laughs with you. Cry and you cry with your girlfriends." —*Laurie Kuslansky*

an even "B"etter Christmas | Selecting the next travel planners was now becoming the most anticipated part of our special Christmas book club nights.

B y the time we held our next Christmas celebration, travel had become an integral part of our group. Traveling together, along with the planning and anticipation of our getaway, had become as much fun as Christmas is to a child. With new members joining throughout the year, and the constant promise of new places to go, there was a lot to celebrate!

Perry, who hadn't planned a trip for the group in four years, was now desperate to be chosen as a planner. She couldn't wait till the time came to select our planners. But there was a twist to this year's process.

> secret agent selection

Pat and another *GG* had planned a surprise method for selecting the next year's planners. They searched the web for some innovative Christmas gift-game ideas and adapted one for the *GG* Christmas night. All that was required was a set of gift-wrapped boxes and a story – simple enough. They went all out by wrapping identically sized boxes in shiny silver foil and tied with blue ribbons. Only two contained Secret Agent buttons inside them. Whoever opened these special boxes would have the task of planning the next year's getaway. The remaining boxes were empty.

" A book is a gift you can open again and again."
—Garrison Keillor

The noise level began to escalate as the selection process was set to begin. The excitement of 'unwrapping' our next trip planner was heightened by the arrival of a *GGB*, with camera in hand, ready to capture the moment. He promptly accused us of breaking the sound barrier while having "too much fun." "Well, that's the point, isn't it?" we shot back. Our goal is to have fun! He did his best, standing on chairs and crouching on the floor, all in the name of capturing us in action.

Next came the story. The example from the web was liberally sprinkled with the words "right" and "left" throughout. The pair customized the story to make the game truly theirs, which made it even more fun. The plan was to assign one of the *GGs* who was unable to travel the next year to read the story. Every time she read the word "right," we would pass our boxes to the right. Similarly, every time she read "left," we would pass our boxes to the left. At the end of the story, everyone would open the gift box she was holding, and the planners for the next getaway would be revealed.

Anxiety and anticipation were building but not all for the same reason. While some *GGs* softly chanted, "I hope I win! I hope I win!" others cried out, "Not me! Not me!" Once the story was finished and the boxes stopped moving, the room filled up with silence. As Perry looked at Pat, she whispered, "Open your box." Pat resigned herself

"Sometimes when I can't sleep, I wonder where we would go if I was planning: Paris? London? San Diego? Montreal? Amsterdam? A spa in the desert? A train ride through the Rockies? A dude ranch in Montana? No, scratch that, I hate horses. I speculate until I drift off to sleep. This is my alternative to counting sheep; I count possibilities for a *GG* getaway destination."
—*Perry*

to the task, and was relieved to announce, "My box is empty!" One by one, we went around the table and revealed the contents of our boxes (empty or not).

Perry's smile deflated like a punctured birthday balloon as she showed us her empty box. Kathleen, oblivious to Perry's plight, had secured one of the coveted Secret Agent buttons in her box and was already attaching it to her top.

The other *GG* that was the lucky winner said, "What are the odds of that? Enough is enough, I planned last year." With a smile on her face, she turned to Perry and dramatically passed the Special Agent button to her. "Take it, it's yours, nobody wants it more than you do." Perry was delighted, jumping at the offer. "I'd love to take the Secret

gg discovery

It's small gestures that strengthen bonds. Like the one in which one GG passed her Secret Agent button to another. A toast to great friends.

· · · · · · · · · ·

Agent button," said Perry, then pinned it on her shirt and happily wore it all night long. See Chapter 5, "*GG Getaways*," for more on why we were thrilled to have Kathleen and Perry planning the next getaway.

› A to Z gift exchange

Our traditional gift exchange (now in its second year) continued with the next letter in the alphabet. The year of Bs brought, among other creative gifts, a stuffed Bad Blue Bird (which recited various insults to any passersby who set off its hidden motion-activated recorder), a blue bag with boob cream and a donation to a breast cancer charity. All were further examples of the great lengths *GGs* are willing to go to when put to the test.

When it was time to go home (hours later...much later), our voices were hoarse from laughter. From this night forward, Perry would speculate no longer when counting destinations to get to sleep; she now had a mission. Where in the world would the *GGs* be going next? We were all holding our breath.

"B" Christmas gifts

leopard **b**lanket

shell **b**ookends

bling watch

GG treasure **b**ox

cheese **b**oard
with spreader

biscotti jar

bling **b**ag with **b**rushes

bad-mouthed **b**lue
bird in a **b**lue **B**liss **b**ag
with **B**liss **b**oob cream

"Polly, our bad-mouthed blue bird, has become part of the *GG* tradition, as she now makes an appearance at every Christmas book club meeting." —*Perry*

Lolita trilogy | Exploring a different media format at our meeting.

> book 1: *Reading Lolita in Tehran*

While we love to have fun during our meetings, there are special nights that strike a chord in all of us, especially when we find books that force us to confront complicated topics. *Reading Lolita in Tehran* by Azar Nafisi was a perfect example and, in the end, it became part one in a trilogy. This night was particularly memorable because it provoked intensely thoughtful discussions.

The book is a memoir of Nafisi's experiences from her life in Iran during the revolution in 1978 to her departure in 1997. It highlights her resistance to following prescribed cultural restrictions, such as submitting to wear a veil, which led to her expulsion as a university professor. We felt particularly connected to the book club that Nafisi formed with seven of her former female students. We learned about the country's political climate through the personal lives of the book club members, who meet weekly at Nafisi's house to discuss controversial works of Western literature. The women are provided with safety under the veil of secrecy and the privacy of Nafisi's home.

As members of a Western society, we are shocked by the plight of these women. They live in a world that is a complete contrast to the freedom we take for granted in our nation. Just the same, we relate to the camaraderie that developed among members in Nafisi's meetings because it seemed to echo that of our own gatherings.

> book 2: *Lolita* by Vladimir Nabokov

Captivated by the complex nuances of the plot and characters of *Reading Lolita in Tehran*, we felt the next book choice – the original *Lolita* – was a natural progression. Even though *Lolita* was first published in Paris in

" The only books that influence us are those for which we are ready, and which have gone a little further down our particular path than we have yet got ourselves." —*E.M. Forster*

1955 and later became a classic, some of us had never read the book. Although we had empathy for Nafisi's book club members, until we had read *Lolita* it was difficult to comprehend the extreme censorship and suppression that Nafisi's group had risked to read this book.

In our discussions about *Lolita*, we agreed unanimously that the premise of the book was the corruption of an innocent child by a calculating adult. As mothers of daughters, this read left us feeling ill at ease at the thought that something like this could happen to a young child.

› movie 3: *Lolita*

True to our book club blueprint, we always discuss the previous month's book club choice when we meet. Changing our format slightly, we viewed the 1997 movie version of *Lolita* to compare the story lines and characters of the movie and book. We were surprised to discover how different our view of the movie was from the book. We collectively felt that the movie portrayed a flawed, yet weak adult being exploited by a deceitful, manipulative child. In fact, this was the antithesis of our impression of the book. And we were astonished at ourselves for feeling empathy for the main character, Humbert Humbert.

As *Lolita* took us on an emotional journey, we looked to, what else, comfort food. Our host served popcorn, a movie tradition, and hot spiked chocolate – perfect companions to the film. **See Chapter 8, "GG Bevies."** But even such comfort was no match for the intense conversation and debate that followed the viewing, and all other details, including the food, became secondary. Indeed, after the last *GG* left the meeting, our host discovered that she had forgotten to set out the appetizers she had prepared that afternoon.

a change of venue | A generous "surprise" gift from one of the *GGBs*.

A s you will quickly learn, the *GGs* typically leap at any opportunity to participate in events as a group, but this one was organized by a *Giller Girl Boy* (*GGB*).

It started with a fundraiser, which gave the husband of a *GG* an opportunity to surprise his wife and all of us. As part of the silent auction program, he bid on a gift certificate for a lingerie store, complete with limousine transportation and champagne! When he won it, our *GG* sister was pleased and even more thrilled when he later announced that the plan was for her to share the prize with all of her *GGs*. A perfect *GG* event promising loads of fun.

› are we there yet?

The *GG*s met at 7 p.m. on a Wednesday evening for this *GG* outing. Within minutes of everyone's arrival, we climbed into a waiting limousine and drove along a country road to a Victorian-inspired village. We arrived in front of a delightful lingerie store. We were ushered inside and welcomed with glasses of champagne and hors d'oeuvres. And there was more. We were the only patrons in the store that evening – the floor was all ours! We were each handed small satin envelopes. "What on earth now?" a delighted *GG* exclaimed.

Each envelope contained a gift certificate for lace luxuries we could purchase in the store that evening. We could hardly believe it. No sooner had one *GG* uttered, "Can it get any better than this?" then we were ushered up a flight of stairs to a room overflowing with silk and lace garments. There were small tables laden with trays of wonderful temptations for the palate as well.

"Does it get any more fun than this; limousine, champagne, lingerie and laughter."

—*a delighted GG*

We sipped and sampled, swapped and swooned, as lace passed between dressing rooms and laughter filled the air. All too soon, our packages had been tied with satin ribbon and our evening had come to a close, but not before we hugged and kissed our hosting *GG* (passing on our thanks to her husband) and reminded ourselves about how lucky we were to have each other.

dessert anyone? | Reading between the wines takes a whole new meaning, all in the name of charity.

As you've undoubtedly already discovered, it doesn't take too much coaxing to get the *GG*s together, and if there's a worthy cause behind the opportunity, well then, all the better. Such was the case with a local Decorate your Dessert Table for Cancer fundraiser. The criteria were perfect for our group: register a table, prepare a simple dessert, decorate the table, invite friends to join you, enjoy your dessert and have some fun – all in the name of the Canadian Cancer Society.

Perry got the ball rolling with a phone call to Kathleen. They met and brainstormed a plan to submit our centerpiece entry. To no one's surprise, they created a book club theme for the table using the *GG* Book Club mantra of "reading between the wines" as inspiration. Books and wine bottles, how could we incorporate them? Kathleen rushed to her basement to retrieve a few wooden wine cases, while Perry scoured the local thrift shop for a well-worn paperback. The concept for the *GG* table was taking form.

They gathered a few wine corks, made a quick trip to the florist, removed pages from an old thrift-shop book and, with the help of a supportive *GGB*, set about putting together a winning centerpiece. Using varying lengths of clear fishing line as thread, they wove the pages from the paperback alternately between the wine corks and strung the quirky results from the

" Life is uncertain. Eat dessert first." —*Ernestine Ulmer*

ceiling. Kathleen loves to hang the unexpected from the ceiling and had used this technique before for many decorating assignments.

All that remained was the assembly. Armed with their props and dessert ingredients, they headed to the venue for the contest. Did we mention there was a prize for the best-dressed table? Never lacking imagination, Perry prepared a spectacular dessert of cheese and fruit served on different laminated copies of our favorite *GG* book covers, with a rich sabayon and fruit parfait to finish. Brilliant! With elegant roses, wine crates, bottles and wine glasses, along with the dangling spectacle of pages and corks, the table came to life, replicating the true spirit of the *GG* Book Club. When the rest of the *GG*s arrived for the evening event they were impressed with their *GG* sisters' creativity. It was truly magnificent.

P.S. The GG table won first prize. But that goes without saying.

bon voyage | bon voi azh | noun; verb

1. > a French phrase that means "good journey"
2. > a salutation used by a *GGB* (Giller Girl Boy) to express fond farewell to his traveling *GG*

bon voyage

· ·

We began as an ordinary book club but our unique format set us apart from others. Although special to us, it wasn't until we added the travel component that our book club became extraordinary.

beginnings:
our travel story

You'll learn how we've added the dimension of travel to our book club experiences. Since our first getaway, the element of surprise has been the cornerstone ingredient. This is how we became a traveling book club.

first steps | Committing to "passports on the table." Little did we know what was in store for us.

We were having a regular book club evening, filled with lively conversation, contagious laughter and our bites and bevies. It had been two years since our book club began and our *GGs* were getting more creative with hosting meetings. Now we were a group of seven, with the addition of a new *GG* who had joined us the previous summer. This was the third time Kathleen played host at her home, and her book selection for the night was *Atonement* by Ian McEwan. In an attempt to theme the evening and offer some clues about her book selection, Kathleen drew ideas from a family cookbook and served a selection of dishes, including her Welsh rarebit, reminiscent of the 1940s. **For the Welsh rarebit recipe as a fondue, see Chapter 7, "GG Bites."**

> "I opened my beloved family cookbook, the dog-eared, well-used one containing my mother's and grandmother's recipes, lovingly detailed in my mother's handwriting."
>
> —*Kathleen*

As the night evolved, one of the *GGs* started to digress with details of a recent vacation. If you haven't already realized, digression is a common practice during our meetings. So, naturally, talk quickly turned to travel, as it so often does. All of our members love to travel, and many have visited exotic destinations in Asia, South America and Europe. Who doesn't love to live vicariously through the travels of good friends?

> let the travel adventures begin

Looking back, it was bound to happen. Spurred on by our love for travel and Perry's keen talent for planning, traveling became part of our lexicon, a lexicon that has expanded with every book and meeting.

Perry had asked the same question during many of our previous meetings: "Why don't we go somewhere together?" This time when she asked there was silence – a commodity used sparingly in the *GG* circle – that echoed while we exchanged glances around the room.

We'd discovered that over the years we all enjoyed each other's company, so a getaway seemed a natural next step. Although we had vacationed with our spouses and/or families, surprisingly, none of us had ever traveled with just girlfriends. Some had reservations, no pun intended, while others were ready to pack their bags.

With the prospect of taking a trip with our book club cohorts on the horizon, we allowed ourselves to envision another type of travel experience. Collectively, the *GGs* could do things their spouses and children would never want to do. What better way to experience such travels than with our fun-loving *GG* sisters?

> passports on the table!

The next thing we heard was Perry making an outrageous suggestion. "Well, if we're going to travel together, then it has to be passports on the table!" she exclaimed. "Passports on the table? What does that mean?" we all replied. Being the adventurer in the group, Perry proposed that we all be prepared to travel to destinations that required a passport and, just for a little extra bravado, only the planners would know the destination. For everyone else it would be a huge surprise.

Fed by visions of fun and unabated travel, the *GG* travel blueprint was born. **See Chapter 10, "Getaway Blueprint."** Like our meetings, where books and agenda are a surprise, similar guidelines shaped the planning of our travels. Let the adventures begin!

as a result of our travel experiences, a *GG* has become...

a trusting, faithful, adventure-driven, life-experienced maven. She has heard personal revelations, experienced middle-of-the-night snoring escapades, and overcome fears and phobias with the support and encouragement of her fellow *GGs*.

selecting the planners | Who was going to plan the *GG* getaways?

We opened the Pinot Noir, set out the bites and got together to discuss putting our "passports on the table," just as Perry had envisioned.

› planner selection

As in our first book club meeting, we needed a volunteer to plan our inaugural surprise getaway. Two hands shot up immediately. You guessed it, party-planner extraordinaire Perry and detail-maven Kathleen. For the next several months, they would become affectionately known as "the planners" to those of us who were going along for the ride.

That night at Kathleen's, the excited chatter typical of our meetings surged and reached a new peak. The discussion questions for the previous month's book selection were abandoned on the coffee table and all attention was directed at the how's and, most importantly, the when's of the proposed travel event. The one thing we all knew for sure was that everyone was in. No one wanted to miss this new and exciting opportunity.

So many decisions had to be made. After we settled the all-important question of who the planners would be, we needed to agree

decisions, decisions

∙∙∙∙∙∙∙∙∙∙∙∙∙∙∙∙∙∙∙∙∙∙∙∙∙

❏ Who will plan the getaway adventure?

•

❏ What are good travel dates?

•

❏ How much do we spend on the getaway?

•

❏ How far do we want to travel?

on the duration of our getaway and sort out everyone's availability. That decision didn't take very long to make either: a weekend – two nights and three days – seemed reasonable, at least for our first trip.

Next up was cost, a subject that unexpectedly invited democracy into the meeting that night. We actually decided how much to spend based on a vote, a rarity within our group. On scraps of paper folded neatly into squares, we each wrote down what we would be willing to spend on a weekend away. We averaged the numbers and, voilà, we had our budget. We agreed to follow whatever payment arrangement our planners deemed appropriate.

The excitement of that evening hung in the air for days as the *GGs* pondered the possibilities of their new adventure. It was clear, though, we had officially become a traveling book club.

"With $600 a person to work with, how on earth were we going to entertain our *GGs* for three days and two nights in any destination? We felt we had a monumental task ahead of us."

—*Perry*

planning the getaway | Getting creative with a very limited budget.

Just to make it all the more fun, the planners decided to build the getaway around the concept of an all-inclusive vacation. Can you remember a time when you weren't responsible for the dinner bill or the cab ride home? It has to be years ago, maybe as long ago as when you were a kid. When we've traveled personally, most of us have had to worry about making hotel reservations and flight arrangements, to say nothing of packing and checking our entire family's luggage. All that would change. Now the shoe was on the other foot.

It would be several months before the group left on their first voyage and our planners were determined to keep everyone guessing right up to the end. The planners got busy planning the details, first with a few phone calls to each other, followed by lunch or coffee meetings or over a glass of wine, thrown in for good measure.

GG getaway mission

To plan a getaway for our book club in the tradition of a great Agatha Christie mystery novel, never knowing what is going to happen the next minute or what will come around the next corner.

This is: a getaway adventure planned for our girlfriends, a fabulous time with no responsibilities.

This means: NOT knowing where we're going or how we're getting there – no directions required.

It also means: not worrying about where we'll sleep or what time we'll eat or what we'll do for fun.

Our goal: to relax and enjoy the fun-filled adventure.

As much fun as the planners were having designing the ultimate getaway, the others – or "hostage *GGs*," as we called ourselves – were having a blast speculating on the final destination. As the heralded weekend approached, the *GGs*' thoughts turned to another dilemma: what to pack. The hostage *GGs* were convinced we'd get a list of activities or at least some clues as to what to bring along at one of the remaining book club meetings before the getaway. The fear of not showing up with the right clothes was growing. In the end, bits and pieces of information were finally revealed, but they were meagre at best. On top of that, the planners told us at the last minute that we had luggage restrictions, and could bring nothing larger than a carry-on bag. Did that mean we were going on a plane?

Among the bits and pieces offered at the last book club meeting before our trip, the group received a "shoe packing list." This curious collection of recommendations was supposed to help us determine what clothing to bring based on the suggested footwear. That was as close as the group was going to get to receiving any details before our weekend. The constant barrage of questions, it turns out, had only served to strengthen the planners' resolve to keep everything a mystery. We were indeed going to be hostages for the weekend, at the total mercy of our planners. What on earth were we going to be doing?

"Never in a million years did we think the planners would be able to keep our destination a secret. We knew we could make them crack under the pressure of questions before the getaway. After all, we would have strength in numbers, especially after a booktini, maybe two. We'd keep pouring until we got our answer."
—a hostage GG

first official getaway | A familiar city delivers exciting firsts.

Our planners, Perry and Kathleen, were nervous. They still had lots of last-minute details to address before the day could unfold smoothly and deliver tons of fun. But for the hostage *GGs*, it felt like Christmas morning. The lot of us were beside ourselves with anticipation, as we jammed our carry-ons into the back of Pat's minivan (she had generously donated it, her status as a hostage passenger notwithstanding). The roles were suddenly reversed. There was nothing we hostage *GGs* could do at this point but sit back and enjoy the ride. Our planners, on the other hand, were now starting to feel the pressure of delivering on the "surprise" they had promised.

Because we were leaving at noon, the planners prepared lunches-on-the-go. Stopping for lunch along the way was not an option because we were trying to beat rush-hour traffic on a Friday afternoon to get to our big-city destination (and we didn't want to be late for our first getaway cocktail hour). This old-fashioned travelling-in-the-car meal reminded many of us of childhood family road trips. But there were no peanut-butter-and-jelly sandwiches, cheese sticks or juice boxes allowed here. This had to be a traveling lunch worthy of the inaugural getaway. **See the Mufflata recipe in Chapter 7, "GG Bites."**

destination:
Toronto, Ontario

# of GGs: 7

mode of travel:
minivan

weather:
pouring rain

driver: Perry

cruise director:
Kathleen

> day 1

As if it wasn't enough that the hostage *GGs* didn't know where they were going, our planners continued to keep our activities a mystery, too. When we first boarded the chariot, each *GG* found an identical box, decorated with cryptic stickers and photos, on her seat. These were Chinese take-out containers – a clue in itself given one of our planned dining excursions – and they ingeniously contained the clues to our trip. What better way to start the getaway than with a box stuffed, in true mystery-book format, with hints about the activities we'd be enjoying during our weekend, to be unravelled along the way. Agatha Christie would have been impressed!

But there was a glitch: we couldn't open up our boxes of clues until the planners gave the signal.

toronto clue box
Container: Chinese take-out box

Clues:	Venue:
Broken china	The Gardiner Museum
Miniature shoes	Bata Shoe Museum, Kensington walking tour
Toy African animals	Ethiopian restaurant
Emery board	Pedicure
Sheet music (cut into pieces)	Reservoir Dance Club
"100" written on paper	Theatre: *Me, Dad and The Hundred Boyfriends*
Tea bag	Red Tea Box restaurant

Numbers on cards: correspond to numbers placed on the beds in the hotel (where the *GGs* would be sleeping)

> are we there yet?

Like children waiting to open their gifts, the hostage *GGs* begged to look into their clue boxes. But Perry and Kathleen resisted. After spending hours creating the clues, they worried their choices might give away the destination and activities too soon. They had managed to keep them a secret for months, after all, to create a sense of suspense (not *The Da Vinci Code* kind of suspense, but pretty good nonetheless). But the moment arrived at last. After a fabulous traveling lunch, and with only

destination possibilities

....

Spa weekend: anywhere

Montreal: maybe too far

Niagara-on-the-Lake: maybe we're going to a play

Stratford: to see a different play

Ottawa: the nation's capital

Toronto: no way, that's too obvious!

an hour left before reaching our destination, the planners held their breath and instructed the girls to tear back the lids on their clue boxes.

As the hostage GGs squealed with laughter, the planners exchanged broad smiles and thumbs-ups from the front seats.

The hostages carefully examined every clue – miniature shoes, a piece of broken china, an African animal, a tea bag and torn pieces of sheet music – with puzzled expressions. Again, the hostages drilled Perry and Kathleen with questions. "Why do we have rubber animals in our boxes?" "What does a broken piece of china have to do with a weekend away from the kids?"

Everyone was so busy speculating about the destination and activities that we missed an important clue – a turn in the road that eliminated the possibility of another potential major destination on our list.

Thanks to the weather – it was pouring rain – and steamy windows, the planners maintained the suspense a little bit longer. Finally, one of the girls stopped talking, eating and speculating long enough to actually look out a window and notice landmarks. After three hours of intended wrong turns, winding country roads and detours, our entourage finally turned off the highway and onto Yonge Street. The mystery was over. We were staying in Toronto.

Perry and Kathleen still worried that the hostage GGs might be a little disappointed with their choice. But it was a brilliant destination. While we were all familiar with the city, or at least thought we were, we still had no idea what was in store for us. And, frankly, it didn't matter where we were going or for how long. It was the sense of excitement of going on an adventure, an adventure with girlfriends, that made all the time spent planning worthwhile.

› reservations, please

While Kathleen checked us in, the hostage *GG*s huddled in the lobby with great anticipation. We looked a bit like elementary schoolchildren waiting for the teacher's next instructions.

But our getaway got off to a dubious start – our hotel reservation was apparently lost. What was a planner to do with no accommodations and seven luggage-wielding *GG*s on a civic holiday weekend? The lineup of guests with reservations was getting longer behind Kathleen. And now people were staring. When Perry arrived back from the parking garage, the situation seemed to escalate. As the hostages waited within eyesight of our planning duo, both of whom practically threw themselves at the hotel staff and begged for help, the whispering got louder.

Kathleen remained resolute, straightened her back, swallowed the lump in her throat and addressed the hotel clerk with uncertainty. "I know you'll be able to help us. Please don't make me walk back to those women and tell them you don't have our reservation." The clerk watched as the sweat trickled down Kathleen's brow. "Just a minute, I'll see what I can do." After all the planning, had it come to this? Homelessness for her *GG*s?

Minutes later, although Kathleen thought the Sistine Chapel had been painted quicker, the clerk came back with some news. His broad smile and wink brought color back to Kathleen's cheeks and stopped her impending heart palpitations. When he handed over multiple sets of keys, the planners shot a swift "don't move" instruction to the hostages, and rushed off to see what kind of accommodation Kathleen had managed to secure. At this point, the size or amount of amenities didn't matter much. The planners would have been happy to share double beds in the basement.

When Kathleen and Perry reached their floor, relief spread like a cloak. The hallway featured elegant carpets and well-decorated walls. And the rooms, well, they were better than any of their wildest dreams. They were presidential. The planners took a few well-deserved minutes to collect their composure and then headed back to the lobby to assemble their *GG*s.

> "On our trips, we want a *GG* to have the time of her life, to build enough memories to fill a journal and to have cheeks that ache from laughter. We want to make memories, great memories, the kind of memories you tell your granddaughter about when you grow old."
> —*Kathleen*

home base

··

In the end, the accommodations were spectacular.

> One room with two double beds and full bath

> One room with a king bed and full bath

> One suite with a living room, dining room and kitchen connecting the two other rooms, with another full bath

Now with smug expressions, Kathleen and Perry escorted the remaining *GG*s to their beckoning quarters. The hostages, of course, were oblivious to the magnitude of the averted crisis.

Giddy with anticipation, Perry and Kathleen opened the double doors to the suite. Everyone ran through interconnecting rooms with child-like enthusiasm. It was like the first day at camp when everybody tries to figure out who would bunk with whom.

> it's in the details

As we checked out the rooms, we were curious about the cards with numbers on the beds.

Kathleen and Perry came up with a system for who would be bunking together. Everyone was told to look in their clue box. They had just enough time to randomly place the numbers on the beds during their quick inspection of the accommodations and now the hostages had to match their number with the number on the bed.

The next order of business – unwinding for an hour or so with some bites and bevies – was upon us. It was only three hours since we had left, and already it seemed like home was a lifetime away.

The planners had decided that since frivolity and friendships were the priority for our getaway, the *GG*s needed to seal this intention with a pledge, an old-fashioned kind of pledge. Their creative juices never ceased to amaze us. Giggling uncontrollably, we grabbed our pens and signed the Passport Pledge. To this day, we still follow it.

The planners wanted to ensure that the events of the weekend were recorded for posterity. But they didn't want just one person taking all the photos. Often the photographer is missing in photographs – think about those old vacation photos when you were never quite sure if Dad was actually there. So our planners introduced the group to the Paparazzi

passport pledge

There is something sacred about a girl's inner circle of friendships. This weekend promises to nurture honesty, strength and trust, and to bestow a lifetime of cherished moments on our *GG* sisters.

- I will share a bed, cold feet and tolerate snoring without complaint.
- I agree to sleep in confined quarters for the designated time without complaint.
- I will not hog all of the blankets...just some.
- I will be allowed one phone call a day, but only for emergencies.
- I will not bring my cell phone or laptop with me.
- I will try not to steal anyone's favorite socks or PJs
- I will not clean up...messy is okay.
- I will share one secret and embarrassing moment without reservation.
- I will not count calories. Indulgence is the law.
- I will function on as little sleep as possible. I can catch up on my sleep when I get home.
- I will allow myself to be photographed anytime "as is." All photos will remain the property of the *GG*s.
- I will be open-minded to all forms of entertainment and food experiences.
- I will be prepared to dance if the situation requires.
- I will keep any *GG* misadventures a secret.

You now qualify for the Passport Pledge Trial Weekend of the Giller Girls.

Date _____

Signature _____

Badge, also tucked away in one of the clue boxes. Kathleen and Perry placed several disposable cameras on the table, along with an agenda that assigned each person (the designated paparazzo) a time slot in which to shoot our adventure together. Another brilliant idea! Everyone would share in the responsibility of capturing the weekend's special moments.

> "I've heard that if you look like your passport photo, you're not well enough to travel. Well, that's not something we're going to subscribe to, is it?" —Pat

> the big reveal

The hostages were hoping to get more clues for the weekend activities during our first cocktail. We did...well, sort of. It wasn't a full agenda, but a *GG* Shoe Itinerary. See example in Chapter 10, "Getaway Blueprint." After all, doesn't everything revolve around shoes? Our job was to match our clothing to our shoes. One of the *GG*s, who had been convinced the getaway was a spa retreat, lamented about the clothes she'd packed. "I have much nicer clothes at home than what I have here!"

The mystery continued, but for Perry and Kathleen, the details, including meal options, activities and venues, were carefully plotted on their Planners' Itinerary. Of course, it was for their eyes only.

> follow that cab

After a relaxing cocktail hour, we were off in our two-inch heels. Nobody was completely sure if they had selected the right outfit to go with their shoes, but we were ready for action, nonetheless.

In the excitement of leaving the hotel for our first planned activity, Kathleen and Perry mistakenly jumped into the same cab, forgetting that no one in the other cab would know where they were going. After a bit of yelling and arm waving, our planners got the message,

day 1 | planned itinerary

10:00 a.m. finish lunch prep
12:00 p.m. departure
2:00 p.m. lunch
4:00 p.m. arrive at Delta Chelsea Hotel
5:00 p.m. bites and bevies
8:00 p.m. Theatre Passe Muraille *Me, Dad and The Hundred Boyfriends*
10:00 p.m. Ethiopian House restaurant
12:00 a.m. back to home base

> NO to returning to home base after dinner. "Just one more" at the Irish Embassy.

but their cab had already sped off. So, with little option, we told the cabbie, "Follow that cab!" Haven't you always wanted to use that line at least once in your life? Needless to say, it became one of our catch phrases for the weekend.

The plan was to fill each day with a variety of activities. On this night it was an incredibly funny show at the Theatre Passe Muraille, then Ethiopian dining (a first for all). But when Kathleen and Perry were ready to call it a night, the rest of the group was confused: "What do you mean there's nothing planned for after dinner?" The planners wanted us to get a good night's rest before heading out for the next full day of events. Serious orders for some serious fun to come.

But a *GG* mantra has always been "just one more," and in the end, tradition prevailed. Someone suggested that we could go to the Irish Embassy. Someone else piped up, "Do you think that we're appropriately dressed for an embassy?" Off we went, explaining en route that the "embassy" was actually a pub.

day 2 | planned itinerary

9:00 a.m.   breakfast in hotel room
10:00 a.m. Kensington Market
            Foodies Walking Tour
11:00 a.m. eat and explore
            Kensington area
12:00 p.m. Elmwood Spa
5:00 p.m.   bites and bevies
7:00 p.m.   dinner options:
            Spring Roll or Kit Kat
            restaurant
9:00 p.m.   dancing at Reservoir
12:00 a.m. back to home base

> NO to both dinner options.
Exhausted, we relaxed at the suite.

> day 2

"Morning so soon?" everyone grumbled. Still, we pulled on our comfortable shoes and hit the pavement. The day began with a Foodies Walking Tour through Kensington Market, a distinctive multicultural neighborhood in downtown Toronto. In fact, in November 2006, the much-celebrated and longstanding market became a National Historic Site. We walked, talked, window-shopped and grazed the aisles for hours. There were endless samplings of Polish, Middle Eastern and Mexican foods, including a new favorite, chili chocolate truffles. This was a great morning of exploring and, of course, we squeezed in a little shopping.

As the truffles made their way through the group in the cheery little chocolate shop, one of the GGs spotted a vintage store a few doors down. In a cleverly executed plan, we managed, one by one, to covertly visit the store. This little retail sideline wasn't on the scheduled tour, but we couldn't pass it up. And the guide hardly missed us because we took turns visiting the shop in groups of two for 10 minutes at a time during the organized walk. You'd have thought it was the first time the GGs have walked through a vintage store. Just about everyone in the group managed to leave with a classic handbag.

spa clues

Clues:	Venue:
Can of Swedish meatballs	Swedish massage
Buddha incense figure	Thai massage
Scented candle	Aromatherapy massage
Stone	Hot stone massage
Toe separators	Pedicures for everyone!

With all that walking, our feet – along with the rest of our body – screamed for relief. Thankfully, our planners timed a spa treatment following our walking tour. Although going to a spa wasn't new for any of us, none of us had ever been to a with a group of seven giggling women before. The two GGs who received a Thai massage are still talking about it today.

Getting all of us booked for the spa was an incredible feat, and it was only accomplished thanks to Kathleen's creative imagination. It's not that simple, after all, to book spa services for seven girls who are to receive their treatments at the same time. Initially, when Kathleen had called the spa (conveniently located beside our hotel) for the booking, the receptionist had told her they were unable to accommodate her request and had suggested we consider another spa. It became apparent that the original plan would need some additional influence. Suffice to say, Kathleen was not above name dropping if it was for a good cause. Our book club was cause enough.

She exclaimed to the receptionist, "These are the Giller Girls. Surely you've heard of the Giller Book prize? There will be seven Giller Girls who would love to visit the spa." Much to Kathleen's astonishment, the receptionist paused briefly and replied, "One moment please, let me see what I can do." Soon, a much friendlier voice returned to the phone. "We would be pleased to make the reservation and we're looking forward to welcoming the Giller Girls on your requested date!"

Did we ever get the royal treatment when we arrived at the spa. As for who was getting what treatment, our planners had devised a plan that was communicated through select items in the clue box. Each clue matched a different spa treatment.

Much to our surprise, we later discovered that the spa thought we were all Giller Book Prize winners traveling together. The sheer misunderstanding of who we were made us giggle all weekend long. We were truly Giller Girls from this day forward.

› voting cards

We got to use voting cards from our clue boxes once during the weekend when deciding between two dinner options. It was a fairly rudimentary tool, but very effective. We simply held up our voting card with the 'yes' or 'no' side showing without explanation or discussion. But the hostage *GGs* confounded the planners on this second night in the hotel, voting 'no' to both dinner choices. We were exhausted. And we had to regain our strength for our evening of dancing. So we decided to kick back instead, relaxing and enjoying some more bites and bevies in our fabulous suite before heading out for the night.

day 3 | planned itinerary

9:30 a.m.   breakfast in hotel room
10:00 a.m. Gardiner Museum –
            teapot exhibition
11:00 a.m. Bata Shoe Museum
2:00 p.m.   Red Tea Box for lunch
4:00 p.m.   drive home
7:00 p.m.   arrive home

> NO to Bata Shoe Museum – our feet couldn't take any more walking.

> book exchange

The planners decided that one of the activities during this weekend would be to discuss our previous book club selection and deliver the next month's book. Never would we have expected this to be an après-dancing activity.

The next book was *The Lovely Bones* by Alice Sebold. We decided to do something a little different with this one – circulate and sign everyone's copy with a personal note that highlighted what the getaway meant to us. Then we broke out the bites and bevies, got into our PJs and began our game of truth or dare. One more opportunity to appreciate the value of the tradition of Commandment #6: "What happens at *GG* Book Club stays at book club."

> day 3

Despite our late night, we had a full agenda the next morning. Our planners were relentless. This time it was a teapot exhibition called The Artful Teapot at the Gardiner Museum. Who knew there could be so many different teapots around the world?

The last scheduled activity for the morning was the Bata Shoe Museum. But with a packed weekend schedule and aching feet, the *GGs* finally cried surrender. The only shoes they wanted to look at were the ones they were wearing. While keeping with our teapot theme, we enjoyed a casual bento box tea lunch at the Red Tea Box before the drive back home. As the elegant bento boxes arrived, our scheduled quick-shot *GG* photographer started taking our last few photos while we sat in the sunshine savoring our final activity together.

This trip began a cherished tradition of travel within our group and the beginning of our *GG* planning blueprint. See Chapter 10, "Getaway Blueprint."

POST CARD

> *toronto post script:*

At the book club meeting following our trip, we reminisced and revisited the fun of our getaway. The planners were presented with awards created by the hostage GGs as an acknowledgment for a job well done. Kathleen and Perry still display their coveted trophies. As it turned out the planners had a surprise as well. Each hostage received a "G" initial charm and bracelet as a memento of their first of many adventures together, and the start of our GG bling tradition.

MESSAGE

ADDRESS

gg getaways

Our *GG* getaways are what make our book club so unique. Building on the success of the inaugural Toronto getaway, we have described four of our extraordinary adventures.

niagara

Niagara-on-the-Lake, Ontario | A long-weekend getaway in picturesque wine country.

Even though we were all eager to embark on our next getaway, we decided to pick a weekend in June to avoid the chilly weather we experienced in May the year before.

Having agreed upon a date for the next getaway, but not a selection process, we were thrilled when two planners volunteered their services. The *GG*s were now getting excited in anticipation of the same great fun we'd enjoyed on our first getaway. We were ready to explore new territories again!

> the plans

Our planners knew what they wanted. Their goal was to offer the hostage *GG*s a refreshing, relaxing venue with some adventure thrown in for good measure. The planning came together effortlessly, as both planners had been to Niagara-on-the-Lake before, but it had been a few years since either had last visited. It was an ideal choice – only a four-hour drive and it had everything – heritage, spas, shopping, world-class vineyards and great food. The organizers' familiarity with the destination, along with a plethora of websites for research, made their planning assignment a snap.

This time, the planners chose not to provide any clues ahead of time or at departure. But it didn't stop the hostage *GG*s from guessing.

As the getaway neared, e-mails flew back and forth among hostage *GG*s' mailboxes. Only three more sleeps,

decisions, decisions

· ·

travel date: mid-June

·

duration: three days, two nights

·

# of GGs: 7

·

budget: based on responsible democratic planning

two more...the anxiety and excitement started to reach a jet plane roar as we checked in with each other to speculate on the details. The last night's sleep became impossible. We were all experiencing the excitement of a five-year-old holding a ticket to Disneyland. It had been a year since the last getaway and we looked forward to an occasion that featured no kids, spouses or work.

> planning challenges

There was one small hurdle in the planning – our accommodations or what we have come to know as our home base, our home away from home. We had so much fun sharing a hotel suite the previous year, but a suite in such a popular destination was definitely out of our budget.

Undaunted, our planners came up with a creative solution. They rented us a fabulous little cottage less than a block from the main street through town. It could not have been more perfect.

> day 1

When we finally congregated for our early-morning departure, the air quivered like a tuning fork with anticipation. The *GGBs* (Giller Girl Boys, our respective partners), whose early-morning job was to deliver each of us to the departure site, looked on with mildly envious smiles. They too had developed a ritual from their wives' traveling group: gathering together for their own evening of dinner, storytelling and fun, often lasting into the wee hours of the night.

We all waited patiently for our ride – a large minivan – to pull into the long driveway. When it had, our *GG* driver jumped out and distributed our Hottie Toddie, **see Chapter 8, "*GG* Bevies,"** and "sticky fingers" (hot cinnamon buns), a local specialty. Next, she opened the sliding door to reveal seven bags bursting with tissue, one on every seat for each *GG*. The *GG* Swag Bag was born! We kissed our boys goodbye and climbed aboard, awaiting permission to open our new bags.

destination guesses
....
Mackinac Island, Michigan

Detroit, Michigan

Niagara Falls, Ontario

Bayfield, Ontario

A spa retreat

destination:
Niagara-on-the-Lake, Ontario
mode of travel:
minivan
weather:
fabulously sunny
driver: Michele
cruise director:
Joan

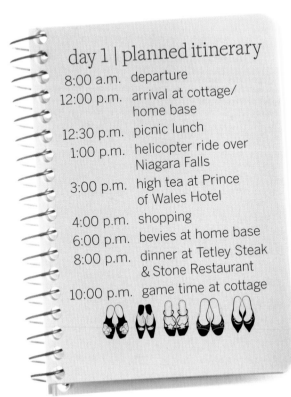

day 1 | planned itinerary

8:00 a.m.   departure

12:00 p.m.   arrival at cottage/
             home base

12:30 p.m.   picnic lunch

1:00 p.m.   helicopter ride over
             Niagara Falls

3:00 p.m.   high tea at Prince
             of Wales Hotel

4:00 p.m.   shopping

6:00 p.m.   bevies at home base

8:00 p.m.   dinner at Tetley Steak
             & Stone Restaurant

10:00 p.m.   game time at cottage

Our *GG* Swag Bag was an actual purse. Stuffed inside was our first official *GG* T-shirt. It was black with the *GGBC* (Giller Girl Book Club) insignia. Although obvious to us, the acronym proved a puzzle to observers. A stranger asked us one afternoon if *GGBC* stood for Girl Guides of British Columbia. Go figure. As a perfect complement to our new ensemble was our latest addition to our *GG* Bing, our YOLO bracelet. You Only Live Once! What a great motto for life.

With the excitement of opening our swag bag, we didn't even notice familiar landmarks fading in the distance. Speculation mounted.

› are we there yet?

As we wound through the countryside it became apparent that we were headed for Niagara-on-the-Lake, also known as Wine Country in Ontario, the perfect spot for our group. For the next three days, we lived by the mantra, "I don't have a care in the world. I'm not a mother or a wife and business is the last thing I'll think about."

As we traveled along our route, laughing, talking and sampling the bites prepared for us, our *GG* driver/planner asked, "Is anybody afraid of heights?" Kathleen froze, muttering under her breath, "Oh my God, what do I say? I have trouble standing on a ladder." Everyone denied any fear of heights. "Now I'm in trouble," Kathleen said to herself. "Do I admit to a lifelong fear or trust my *GGs*?" Her hand flew into the air and she shrieked "I don't do ladders!"

One of our planners responded with a crestfallen "oh," and Kathleen quickly tried to gain valuable peer ground. "Anything other than a ladder will be fine!" She didn't want to dampen the spirit of her beloved planners who had worked so hard. After all, this weekend was in part about building trust among *GG* sisters.

› it's all in the details

The charm of the quaint town revealed itself as the van approached Niagara-on-the-Lake. We passed glorious hotels resplendent with cascading flowers from every windowsill. One more turn off the main street and we had arrived.

We unloaded onto a grassy lane leading up to a cottage, a place all to ourselves. This was ideal for our group – no need to be shushed in the early-morning hours by other hotel guests.

Soon those among the hostages who fashioned themselves as the party hostesses busied themselves with the preparation of a celebratory first cocktail as we waited for the key to arrive. A soft, filtered sun above the canopy of trees highlighted the grass and perennials surrounding us, a scene which seemed to have been lifted from the pages of *Anne of Green Gables*. A delicious lunch appeared from the bountiful hamper pulled from the back of the van onto the lawn. Soon the *GGs* were scooping fabulous chicken salad onto paper plates underneath the arbor in the backyard. **For recipe, see Chapter 7, "GG Bites."** Just as we finished up, one of the planners announced: "Okay, everybody! Back in the van! We'll get the key later."

> "No matter how pleasant the day or venue, a glass of wine promises to complete the picture." —*Pat*

There was a sharp turn in the winding road and we could see a sign up ahead that read: Helicopter Rides 300 feet. Remembering the question about heights, Kathleen suddenly gasped and the hair stood up on the back of her neck. Oh my God, she thought. We must be doing THAT! The ladder was small potatoes compared to what was in store for Kathleen and our group.

"Don't worry, girls. We're going to be together," said one of our planners. "There are two helicopters ready to take us over Niagara Falls."

Not only was the group climbing to altitudes close to the heavens, but the small helicopter would be flying over water. For Kathleen, that meant two worries – the height and depth (she couldn't swim well enough to get to the deep end of a pool let alone save herself from the turbulent waters of the Niagara River).

There's no doubt about it, Niagara Falls is one of the world's most spectacular views from any vantage point. But witnessing tons of water crashing over the earth's rocky edge from the windows of a helicopter is spellbinding. In spite of her original trepidation, Kathleen later told the group that she felt a sense of accomplishment as the helicopter tilted and spun through the air. Indeed, she said she couldn't help but think about the anxiety the New World explorers might have felt as they canoed along the beautiful Niagara River only to find themselves facing this avalanche of powerful waterfalls. Poor them: they had no *GG* planner blazing the trail.

gg discovery

As the unpacking took place, the tradition of sharing and swapping began. It didn't matter who brought an item; the bigger question was who would need it.

· · · · · · · · · ·

Back in the van with a new sense of bravado, the *GGs* sang gratitude to the planners. We'd all seen Niagara Falls before, but none of us had ever seen it from the air.

› home base...finally

Back "home," we discovered our quaint cottage was furnished with the type of vintage décor you'd find in the home of a favorite, albeit eclectic, aunt. We loved everything about it. Even the earthy damp warmth as we threw open the windows brought back childhood memories of our summer vacations.

We quickly moved through the house in search of our sleeping quarters. They were upstairs, "cozy and quaint," which was *GG* code for small and closetless (in keeping with tradition, we later drew numbers to determine who got which bed). But that didn't matter – the landing at the top of the stairs became our communal dressing room. Perry was instantly pleased with the size of the fridge: "Great," she said. "It's large enough for all our bevies." And one of our planners loved the dining room table, roomy enough for our crowd of seven. "We'll have lunch here tomorrow," she said. Soon, the sound of a cork popping was followed by the clinking of glasses as we issued toasts all around.

No time to get too comfortable. The planners had plans. After our adrenaline rush, we were instructed to wear sophisticated but comfortable shoes, since we needed to walk to our next activity. We had reservations for high tea at the Prince of Wales Hotel. We sipped exotic loose leaf teas from around the globe and nibbled on delicate finger sandwiches and fine pastries amidst opulent décor that was reminiscent of the Victorian era. This tranquil, majestic dining room at high tea provided a sharp contrast in surroundings to the breathtaking heights over the falls.

Later that night following dinner, after tossing our high heels aside, we started a new tradition. The planners of the next trip (they were the only ones who had yet to organize a getaway) presented each girl with a pair of matching pajamas, much to the surprise of the planners. We excitedly donned our new PJs and brought out a board game – Taboo (another first), which we played late into the night. One last surprise that night was a chili truffle chocolate on our pillows, the same chili truffles that we had first experienced and loved in Toronto on our last getaway. Our planners had thought of even the smallest touches.

> day 2

We had a packed day of activities, including spa treatments ranging from hot stone massages to aromatherapy

day 2 | planned itinerary

8:30 a.m.	breakfast at home base
9:00 a.m.	walk to spa at Pillar & Post Hotel
12:30 p.m.	impromptu lunch at Shaw Café and Wine Bar
2:00 p.m.	Royal George Theatre
6:00 p.m.	bevies at home base
8:00 p.m.	dinner at Peller Estates Winery
10:00 p.m.	games at home base

day 3 | planned itinerary

9:00 a.m.	departure
10:00 a.m.	breakfast en route
2:00 p.m.	home, safe and sound

facials. The spa was a perfect pursuit, as we needed to recover from the previous evening's game night and prepare for the next match-off. We spent the entire post-spa afternoon in our yoga pants and signature *GGBC* (Giller Girl Book Club) T-shirts, wandering through the picturesque streets of Niagara-on-the-Lake. This prompted many queries from strangers who regarded our matched-uniformed procession through the town's most charming homes and gardens quizzically. Our planners orchestrated our leisurely stroll, taking us by some quaint shops that we naturally felt compelled to investigate.

"A journey is best measured in friends, rather than miles."
—*Tim Cahill*

Although we were still in our *GGBC* T-shirts and glowing from our morning spa treatments, the planners had organized an afternoon treat. Niagara-on-the-Lake is well known for its Shaw Festival, the only festival in the world devoted to the production of plays by George Bernard Shaw. We had matinee tickets for a performance at the Royal George Theatre, one of the festival's three stages that present plays at the Shaw Festival. While the Royal George has a modest exterior, its interior – showcasing Edwardian gilt moldings, red walls and golden lions – was breathtaking. The theatre was originally built as a vaudeville house to entertain the troops during the First World War. It was an appropriate setting for the play we saw, *Waiting for the Parade*, the story of five Calgary women responding to civilian life during the Second World War.

Later that evening, we were instructed to be at the front door by 7:30 with our "best" shoes on. After much swapping of clothes and accessories, we were there, overjoyed with excitement for what promised to be a spectacular night. And our expectations were confirmed when we pulled up to the front doors of the Peller Estates Winery, a French château-style estate. An integral part of the property is the Peller Estates Winery Restaurant, which overlooks the vineyards. It's warm, friendly ambiance made it easy for us to relax and enjoy the seasonal menu and expert wine pairings. As we were ushered to our table by the maître d', the sparkle of the chandelier paled in comparison to our bright smiles. There was no doubt about it – as self-proclaimed foodies, we would count the six-course dinner at the Peller Estates as a major highlight of the entire weekend. It was a dining experience long to be remembered.

› day 3

These precious days came to a close as we slowly rallied for an early-morning coffee together. Although the bags had been packed the night before in preparation for an early start, we always seem to move much slower on the last day of our getaways – and this one was no exception. To brighten our spirits and give us strength for the ride home, the planners squeezed in one more stop – breakfast at a village diner on the way home.

POST CARD

› *niagara-on-the-lake post script:*

Although each GG getaway has been filled with adventure and excitement, this one was particularly special for Kathleen. Together, with the help of her GGs, she conquered a lifelong fear of heights.

For their extraordinary planning, the planners were rewarded with additional charms for the bracelet they received after the Toronto getaway.

MESSAGE

ADDRESS

pelee island

Pelee Island, Ontario | An island getaway featuring a renowned literary guest.

This getaway was based on *The Pelee Project*, a book that we had read during the year since our last getaway. Author Jane Christmas is a journalist who, with her daughter, had taken a break from urban life and traveled to this island to spend the winter.

The planners thought that this would be a perfect opportunity to combine a book read at book club with our getaway travels. It also worked nicely because Pelee Island is only about a two-hour drive from home. This was our third traveling experience, and our planners decided it was time to take the mode of transportation up a notch, no more minivans. We were going to travel in style, by limo!

decisions, decisions
· ·
travel date: mid-June

·

duration: three days, two nights

·

# of GGs: 7

·

budget: based on responsible democratic planning

> the plans

For the first time there were three planners, the last remaining GGs to orchestrate a getaway. One of our planners was of Irish descent and produced the clues for this getaway fashioned in true Irish style – she wrote a limerick, conceived of during her daily walks with her dog – to help guide us along.

At the last meeting before the getaway, we were unceremoniously handed a green trash bag with instructions from the planners that this was a mandate for light packing. The clever limerick provided the compulsory shoe information. Each traveler was invited to bring along a bite, her own signature hors d'oeuvre to be shared at the final destination. This has become a *GG* tradition.

The *GGs* were greeted with florescent life jackets and well-worn paddles as they met at the departure location. Could we really be going camping and canoeing? Tell us it isn't true…but the planners, of course, refused to divulge details. The hostage *GGs* were asked to place their trash bag luggage in the open trunk of the waiting limo.

› day 1

Pat was one of the planners this time and her daughter Dayna, one of our *GGDs* (Giller Girl daughters) had compiled a CD for our road trip, complete with

gg limerick

There are seven women called Gillers,
Who travel far and wide to be thrillers.
Their next trip is an event,
That may involve a big tent.
However one problem prevails,
Causing all sorts of wild tales.
Asking us to pack light in the 'green'
Makes everyone want to scream!
Joan, don't worry you won't be seen
As the GGs go traveling to be Gillers.

"What about shoes?" cried Kathleen,
"I know we must pack very lean!"
Perry asked "Are our toes in or out?"
And Michele inquired, "Would heels be way out?"
Eileen turned with a wink,
Said she would think
Shoes should be two
And comfort is the clue.
So girls pack some flats,
Good for walking in capri slacks.
As the GGs get out to be seen.

Now Pat cried "That's it!
One more clue do you git."
The Margaret gala is not fussy,
So don't dress to be a hussy,
Arrive at MM's by nine.
Traveling must be on time.
So please hold on tight,
As to enjoy our brief flight
As the GGs go traveling to be Gillers.

destination:
Pelee Island,
Ontario

mode of travel:
limo, ferry, taxis

weather:
hello sunshine

cruise directors:
Mary Margaret,
Pat & Eileen

inspirational tunes. Her song selections gave further clues about the destination and it became a new tradition for future road trips.

> GG swag bag

Pretty pink bags awaited us on our seats. One of the *GGs* plucked a string of faux pearls from the bag. "Look what I found! More *GG* bling to add to our collection." As each *GG* followed suit, she found an eclectic mix of terry towels, beaded scarves and cocktail napkins. Now we were even more confused. What kind of escapade was in store for us?

> are we there yet?

We were traveling in style, enjoying decadent cinnamon rolls, all the while wondering why they were being served on Christmas napkins. It all made sense when we discovered that the napkins were actual clues. The laughter subsided as the limo came to a stop at the ferry terminal in Leamington, Ont. There could only be one destination now: Pelee Island.

Just as we were wondering what the ferry passengers would say about our trash bags, the limo's trunk opened to reveal seven fabulous new travel totes, the ultimate of all *GG* Swag Bags. Frenzied repacking of sandals and high heels, belts and scarves into the new bags ensued. We had a ship to catch and no time to fold or smooth out clothing. Some items became a jumbled heap in the confusion. Later that night, one of the girls paraded a pair of underwear that she had found lying unclaimed on the sidewalk, apparently lost in the shuffle of repacking.

The crossing between Leamington and Pelee Island, a mere one-and-a-half hours, was an ideal opportunity for some *GGs* to take a "Perry nap," known to others as a catnap, to make up for lost sleep the night before our long-awaited getaway. In keeping with our tradition of bringing bites along, Perry brought her renowned mango shrimp dish. On a plate the size of a turkey platter, she had organized enough shrimp to sustain her traveling GGs. Imagine the curious stares as Perry boarded the ship balancing her platter on one hand like a waitress. It was just one more example of the lengths we go to just to provide refreshments.

When we disembarked, a large group of women gathering near the terminal met us. The planners had chosen a women's retreat for our group's surprise. The retreat's welcome banner flapped in front of the registration table across from the dock, detailing a few of the activities, but revealing none of our plans. We would be spending some quiet time getting back to basics, the same as Jane Christmas had intended in her Pelee project.

pelee island clue box (GG swag bag)

Container: Pink gift bag

Clues:	Venue:
Pearls wrapped in Christmas paper	Book author's name (Jane Christmas)
Towels, facecloth (GG embossed)	Cottage didn't provide linens
Sheer scarf with beads	Required for belly dancing lesson
Bright triangular scarf	Required for opening ceremony
Napkins with geese	Tin Goose restaurant
Christmas napkins	Again for the author

GG Bling – string of faux pearls, to be worn all weekend long!

› planning dilemmas

We were waiting for a taxi when we were suddenly greeted by a woman opening the back of a well-used van. "Are you the ladies that need a taxi?" she asked. We were speechless as we glanced at the van's interior, which was layered with inches of silt and dust kicked up by the unpaved roads of the island. It was Kathleen, speaking for us, who told the driver, "Oh, that's okay. We'll wait for another taxi." "This is it, the only one on the island," the driver offered with a shoulder shrug. Humbled by the dilemma, we meekly entered the van and placed our

day 1 | planned itinerary

9:00 a.m.	limo to Leamington
12:00 p.m.	enjoy a packed lunch
1:30 p.m.	ferry to Pelee Island
7:00 p.m.	dinner at Tin Goose
9:30 p.m.	join retreat ceremony

day 2 | planned itinerary

8:00 a.m.	bakery breakfast delivery
9:00 a.m.	belly-dancing lessons
12:00 p.m.	lunch at Total Recall Pavillion
1:00 p.m.	Tao of Sex discussion
7:00 p.m.	gala dinner with Margaret Atwood

luggage on our lap, hoping to protect our new bags from the vehicle's grime. We bounced along the dirt road, kicking up enough dust to cause a fog inside the van.

› home base

The taxi ride lasted only a few minutes before we reached our modest cottage, Harmony House. Secluded on the lake with a deck stretching over the water's edge, the cottage was a perfect home base for our getting-back-to-basics theme. We could hear the loons while we unpacked our bags. As we toured the house and looked for our bedrooms using our traditional numbering system, we caught a glimpse of a family of ducks paddling along the lake's edge. Maybe remote wasn't so bad after all.

Situated at the southernmost point of Canada, Pelee Island features 10,000 acres of idyllic vineyards, farms, beaches, parks and forest. There are roughly 150 permanent residents there, many of whom Jane Christmas got to know well during her Pelee project.

› it's all in the details

The map the planners had used to organize the activities left the impression that walking would be the best method of transportation on the island. It seemed a reasonable premise. After all, the island is only nine miles (14.5 kilometers) long by 3.5 miles (5.5 kilometers) wide. In lieu of attending the official opening ceremonies of the retreat, our first activity was dinner at the Tin Goose. The plan was to join the opening ceremonies in progress. But a leisurely stroll after dinner while balancing on stilettos on gravel roads loomed as anything but leisurely. The planners quickly rethought their footwear choices for the weekend in light of the absence of paved roads and sidewalks on Pelee.

A few minutes later on our precarious perambulation, we caught sight of figures moving in the darkness on the far side of a field. We were told that this was the location of our next activity. There we stood in a grassy field in the midst of a Tibetan prayer flag ceremony as women in flowing white gowns with ribbons in their hair chanted. A large ring of lanterns was arranged on the ground to form an illuminated circle of new moons. We approached the lanterns as best we could in stilettos on soft, uneven grass while the women offered to "smudge us" with soot from glowing candles. Uncomfortably we declined. Although we found ourselves a little bit out of place, we were welcomed with a generous spirit. The ceremony lasted well into the night, and was followed by outdoor camping for most of the attendees. Our planners didn't intend for us to stay the night – after all, we had our home base by the lake awaiting us. But there was a glitch – there was no taxi service on the island after 8 p.m. With no street lighting, how far could stilettos get you on gravel roads, anyway? Where was that limo when we really needed it?

How lucky we were to experience island hospitality and be graciously offered a ride to our door from the waiter who had served us earlier that night at the Tin Goose restaurant in town.

> now I lay me down to sleep

As we headed for our bedrooms, we were reminded once more of the special bond we share. There, on each bed, lay a pair of beautiful silk pajamas. Not just any pair of pajamas. Kathleen had hand-selected each colour and size to be a perfect match for each of her *GG* sisters while on a recent trip to Thailand.

> day 2

Because the island is so remote and the ability to transport food so limited, the planners had to be very resourceful when organizing meals. For breakfast, they had arranged for the local bakery to deliver ham and cheese croissants! Imagine greeting the bakery owner in our new silk jammies and faux pearls.

gg discovery

When breakfast is served hot from a local baker no one seems to count the calories.

· · · · · · · · · ·

The day's activities were divided into two sessions the planners signed us up for ahead of time. What girl wouldn't enjoy belly-dancing lessons? (that explained the scarf with beading clue). After lunch, we were treated to a discussion on Taoist sex practices (what girl couldn't learn something new from that topic!?).

Later in the afternoon, we reconvened at Harmony House for a little meditation and some bevies to remember the day's activities. Listening to the loons and watching the ducks drift by on the lake was the perfect backdrop to this contemplative exercise.

> and there was more ·

Along with the retreat group, we were being treated to dinner at the Pelee Island Winery. The island has a long history of producing fine wines. In fact, the wine industry began in 1860, then went on a hiatus for more than a century until 1980, when it was revived again. Lucky for us.

The guest speaker at dinner was Margaret Atwood, a renowned Canadian author, poet, novelist, literary critic, feminist and activist. Just as Ms. Atwood entered the dining room near the table reserved for the *GGs*, Kathleen turned to peer around the room. With shock in her voice and a deer-in-the-headlights expression on her face, she remarked, "Margaret! Hi, what are you doing here?" What could have been an embarrassing moment for Kathleen turned out to be the highlight of her weekend. Equally as surprised by such a reaction, Ms. Atwood responded, "I'm here to speak to your group tonight!"

We couldn't believe our eyes and ears. Margaret Atwood, an author whom we all had respected for more than two decades, was going to address us. Unbeknownst to us, she makes Pelee Island her part-time home. It's not difficult to see how this idyllic and remote setting inspires her writing. We were delighted by her wit and humor that night as she read to us from her new work, *Oryx and Crake*. It added a new layer of appreciation for such an iconic author.

POST CARD

> *pelee island post script:*

The limousine transportation scored huge and we continued the tradition in subsequent getaways. Like Jane Christmas we were grateful for what Pelee Island helped us rediscover, that is, to slow down the pace of life and enjoy it. Our added bonus was the opportunity to meet Margaret Atwood.

MESSAGE · ADDRESS

new york

New York City, New York | Living life large in the Big Apple.

Passports on the table! This was a five-day getaway and we were traveling by air. That much had been revealed by the planners. Five days provided the five GGs making this trip with more opportunities for adventure. But it also introduced a new challenge: could we survive so many days of GG frivolity? The planners for this getaway were chosen at the retro Christmas party and Perry, Kathleen and Pat were the hostage GGs.

> the plans

Previous getaways found us scrutinizing our shoe packing list, or a GG limerick for clues to our getaway destination, but for this trip we were met with deafening silence. We got our only clue one week before departure. The planners invited us for a cocktail rendezvous. While sipping martinis in a lounge high above our city of Sarnia with a magnificent view of the St. Clair River, we finally got some insight when they handed us our GG Swag Bags. Mind you, it wasn't much, considering the bizarre array of items it contained. What could a can of Spam mean? Did a series of numbers represent an area code? Apple socks? That didn't help much!

We had strict instructions by the planners to be at the GG departure sight at 8 a.m. on a day later the next week. Along with our GGBs, the GG daughters witnessed our exodus and chronicled it for future photo albums. Perhaps they were planning for their own future getaways.

decisions, decisions
. . . .
travel date: mid-May

·

duration: five days,
four nights

·

# of GGs: 5

·

budget: based on
responsible democratic
planning

With three traveling templates to work with, we had a successful formula already in place. Again, we were traveling by limousine, at least for part of the way. And we always departed wearing our *GG* Rethink Target T-shirts, and comfortable yoga pants or denim, our typical traveling 'uniform.'

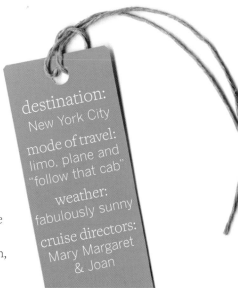

destination:
New York City

mode of travel:
limo, plane and
"follow that cab"

weather:
fabulously sunny

cruise directors:
Mary Margaret
& Joan

> day 1

This time, the limousine took us across the border into the United States and dropped us off at the Detroit airport. Although we still had no details about our final destination, it became apparent as we checked our bags. The destination sign at the airline counter flashing New York, New York gave it all away. This was our first international getaway – the Big Apple, we were ready for it.

> home base

We know that hotel real estate demands a high price in New York City, but that didn't deter the planners from finding perfect accommodations for this trip. We would be enjoying a remarkable hotel suite in Times Square. Like the Red Square in Moscow, Trafalgar Square in London and Tiananmen Square in Beijing, Times Square has achieved the status of iconic world landmark with its animated, digital advertisements. Where else could the *GGs* possibly stay on their getaway to New York City but at this buzzing, glowing, vibrating hub?

The size, location and amenities of our hotel were beyond anyone's expectations. When we stepped off the elevator and turned the corner, double doors greeted us, proving that size can matter! The 916-square-foot suite had an incredible panoramic cityscape view of New York. Securing this kind of real estate for the weekend was an astonishing feat, even for our *GG* planners.

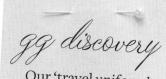

gg discovery

Our 'travel uniform' helps bond us. Plus, it provides instant head counts – the GGs can be as difficult to gather as a herd of cats, especially when they go shopping.

· · · · · · · · · ·

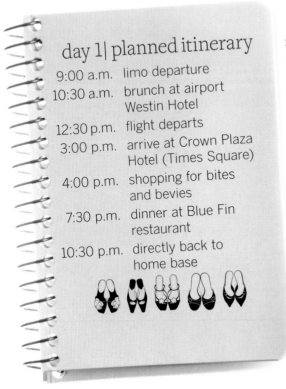

day 1 | planned itinerary

9:00 a.m.   limo departure

10:30 a.m. brunch at airport
            Westin Hotel

12:30 p.m. flight departs

3:00 p.m.   arrive at Crown Plaza
            Hotel (Times Square)

4:00 p.m.   shopping for bites
            and bevies

7:30 p.m.   dinner at Blue Fin
            restaurant

10:30 p.m. directly back to
            home base

This called for celebration (okay, so we'll make any excuse to raise a toast). With a quick trip to a wine merchant and the local deli, we were ready for our first cocktail hour. The suite was perfect. It came complete with a comfy seating area, dining table and a perfect little bar area with small fridge, microwave, coffee maker and mugs, plus lots of wine glasses and other bar accessories. Everything we needed for our entertaining needs.

> on the town

Our first shoe clue for the evening was stilettos, prompting us to rummage through our luggage for the appropriate attire. Zealous *GG* swapping began as one piece of clothing quickly replaced another until the perfect outfits came together. Why is it that an outfit that seems perfect when you're packing it never seems to work when you unpack it? Thank goodness for the *GGs'* sharing policy!

As dinner ended, we were informed that we would be retiring to our home base. What, no after-dinner entertainment? There was a good reason: We had a 4:30 a.m. wake-up call. "Good God, what could they possibly have planned for us?" we grumbled as we left the restaurant and strolled back to the hotel. To our adventurous hearts' content, we learned that we were heading, at an insanely early hour the next morning, to a taping of the *Today* show.

› day 2

The planners had thought of everything. Before our trip, they even prepared a banner for us to display, if by chance, the camera scanned us in the crowd outside the studio. Now it became clear why we had to be there at the crack of dawn. We needed to secure a premium spot at the front of the crowd to display our sign – a spot that might ensure a conversation with any *Today* show host or celebrity. Although new host Meredith Vieira was still weeks away from taking her post, her first appearance was being eagerly anticipated. We proudly displayed our welcome message on our banner.

Amidst the crush of people vying for a perfect spot, we secured a position in the front row. But we didn't expect what was to come. Having donned our recognizable matching *GG* black T-shirts and faux pearls, we were delighted when weatherman Willard Scott introduced us on the air before his centenarian birthday segment. Little did some of us know that our daughters back home had been instructed to record the day's broadcast. Unknown to us, our families were already aware of our new celebrity status.

We chatted with actor Kelsey Grammer, who was being interviewed on the show that day as he graciously autographed our banner. We had to pinch ourselves to make sure this moment was really happening. Once our TV cameo ended and stardom wore off, we hit the streets of New York.

day 2 | planned itinerary

4:30 a.m.	wake-up call
5:15 a.m.	leave hotel
5:30 a.m.	arrive at *Today* show
9:30 a.m.	double-decker bus tour, breakfast (Ground Zero, Century 21 Dept. Store)
12:00 p.m.	lunch at Gobo restaurant
1:00 p.m.	Canal Street (for shopping)
6:00 p.m.	back to hotel – change, bites and bevies
8:00 p.m.	dinner at Picasso restaurant

> it's a sighting

Our first stop was St. Patrick's Cathedral. We had to take turns because our water bottles and bags were not allowed in the cathedral. Minutes after the first group of three entered, they could hear whispers rising up around them. Strangers approached, and asked, "Were you on the *Today* show this morning?" We couldn't believe it – they were talking about us. We found it difficult to contain our excitement as we were shushed by other visitors. To this day, shushing has become the bane of our existence when we gather together to enjoy any kind of group activity.

The remaining *GG*s waiting outside didn't believe the story until they entered the cathedral themselves. Minutes later, they emerged to repeat a similar tale. Not only did we have our 15 minutes of fame with Willard Scott, but we also enjoyed our own celebrity sighting. This was going to be the best *GG* getaway ever. Was the universe speaking to us, trying to tell us something? Was there something bigger in store? Maybe.

gg discovery

Expanding your horizons means finding book club sisters everywhere, even in the most unlikely places.

· · · · · · · · · ·

The day continued with a hop-on-hop-off city bus tour. We longed to see the sites and, of course, we felt compelled to visit Ground Zero.

> a second sighting

Naturally, we approached Ground Zero somewhat apprehensively, and experienced a rush of melancholy once we were there. During our respectful visit, two gentlemen approached us and once again we heard the question, "Were you on the *Today* show today?" This couldn't be happening: two celebrity sightings within 30 minutes of each other! Their wives joined them and shared the excitement of meeting us. We discovered they were fellow Canadians from Calgary, also visiting New York City for the weekend. We explained the details of our adventure, and it was as if we had become instant best friends.

They wanted to hear all about our book club and the balance of activities we had planned for our visit. Of course, only our planners could reveal our itinerary – and only if our new friends promised not to divulge details to the hostages. Our two planners took them aside and whispered their plans for attending a play the next night. We heard the squealing of laughter – as (we later discovered) the Calgary girls delighted in learning that we were all going to watch the same play on the same night! With hushed voices, they promised the planners that their secret was safe with them. Was the universe speaking to us a second time?

> day 3

The *GGs* have always loved to shop, but this day's shopping spree was really something special. We were participating in a two-hour Shop Gotham walking tour featuring local designers and unique shops, the likes of which we would never have found on our own. Our guide made an apology for a slight digression as we made a stop at a store boasting "the world's best rice pudding" for a quick sample. Only in New York City could you expect to find a store that sold nothing but rice pudding. As the morning came to an end we found ourselves at the Union Square Café for lunch. It started to rain, but our spirits could not be dampened as we raised our glasses in a toast to the planners.

Later that evening we would discover what the can of Spam clue meant. We were going to watch the play *Spamalot*. During intermission, we were in the typical ladies' restroom lineup, when there was a huge surprise. Out of the blue, our new 'best' friends from Calgary appeared in line behind us. They had searched every ladies' restroom in the theatre looking for us. They wanted to learn everything about our book club. As we stood in line, we jokingly remarked that maybe we needed to write a book detailing our methods and escapades, and the Calgary girls quickly agreed.

day 3 | planned itinerary

11:00 a.m.	Shop Gotham tour
2:15 p.m.	lunch at Union Square Café
7:00 p.m.	pick up theatre tickets
8:00 p.m.	Spamalot
10:00 p.m.	Sardi's restaurant for late dinner

day 4 | planned itinerary

9:00 a.m.   breakfast
10:00 a.m.   free time shopping
2:00 p.m.   return to home base
3:30 p.m.   leave for theatre
6:30 p.m.   post-theatre drinks
8:00 p.m.   dinner at Balthazar

day 5 | planned itinerary

12:00 p.m.   brunch: The Met
              Museum Petrie
              Court Café
2:30 p.m.   return to hotel in cabs
3:30 p.m.   leave hotel for airport
6:00 p.m.   plane departs

Although we did not see them again, we hope they started their own book club. The universe had spoken to us for a third time and now a plan had been seeded to create this book!

> day 4

A 9 a.m. start launched a leisurely day with free time to shop. This was an opportunity to put what we had learned on our shopping tour to work.

Cabs were hailed, shopping ensued, packages were collected and a quick lunch was consumed along the way. Did we mention Canal Street? It used to separate cannoli from chop suey – Little Italy from Chinatown. And it's the mecca for knock-off handbags and bling, a totally iconic New York shopping experience where you're required to haggle relentlessly to score the best price. Here, we bought our New York *GG* Bling: matching faux circle diamond necklaces. We definitely felt like New York was ours for the taking. As the activities continued throughout the day, our cheeks hurt from laughing and even the occasional "shushing" from the sidelines didn't diminish our spirits.

> day 5

It would have been difficult to be in New York City and not visit at least one of the spectacular museums the city has to offer. Our planners made an excellent choice with the Metropolitan Museum of Art as our final destination. The "Met" is located on the eastern edge of Central Park, along what is known as Museum Mile. It has a permanent collection containing more than two million works of art. One of its exhibits, "AngloMania: Tradition and Transgression in British Fashion," beautifully summed up our theme of fashion during our trip in the Big Apple. Lunch in the Petrie Court Café at the end of our tour was a peaceful way to end a wonderful getaway. A toast to the planners!

POST CARD

CANADA 1 CENT

> *new york*
post script:

It was our destiny; it increasingly seemed, to write about the adventures of the GGs. We made a decision on this trip that we would find a way to share our experiences with other women by writing about our traveling book club. Motivated by messages from the universe, we began the journey to write our book.

MESSAGE　　　　　　　　　　**ADDRESS**

Vancouver, British Columbia | An action-packed West Coast adventure.

v a n c o u v e r

F or the first time ever, passports on the table meant an entire week away. Perry and Kathleen would be reprising their roles as planners. We held our breath in anticipation of the activities that they would offer us.

Six of us would be participating on this trip, including a new *GG* member who had joined the club earlier in the year. Tales of past getaways had fully prepared her for the exciting adventures we had in store. And even though she might have been just a tad worried, she bolstered her courage and announced, "I'm ready for anything!"

› the plans

Perry and Kathleen had been planners before, but choosing a destination – even for the most seasoned *GGs* – is never easy. Over a glass of wine, or maybe a few, Perry and Kathleen listed all their favorite cities and their potential offerings.

Because our getaway was going to be seven days, the longest excursion to date, there was a possibility that we would be traveling to an international destination and the "passports on the table" concept re-emerged as a reality. The time frame made it even more difficult to narrow down the choices, as the options seemed endless. Our planners were torn between a tempting European destination and an exciting North American option.

The choices were narrowed down to the urban excitement of London in the United Kingdom and Canada's outdoor paradise, the Vancouver-Whistler area.

decisions, decisions

· ·

travel date: July

·

duration: seven days, six nights

·

of *GGs*: 6

·

budget: based on responsible democratic planning

Our planners recalled that some *GG*s mentioned they had never been to Vancouver, while most of us had been to London. Were the *GG*s trying to influence the planners? Hmmm, our planners each had a daughter living in Vancouver, so if the West Coast city became our destination, they could enlist help from the two people closest to them who truly understood the importance of a *GG* getaway. It was finally decided: Kathleen and Perry would show us the Vancouver that they knew and loved, with the assistance of their "onsite" help. They just hoped no one would be disappointed about not going to olde London Towne.

Even though the two planners had a good working knowledge of the city, it was a huge bonus to have their daughters available as their on-the-ground crew guiding them in selecting the must-dine-in restaurants and must-go-to places. Because Pat's son lived in Whistler, he was recruited as the on-the-ground crew member for the Whistler portion of the getaway. What a perfect surprise for her.

Kathleen and Perry typically spent weeks researching and planning every minute detail of their getaway, but on this excursion they organized the entire trip during a couple of all-day marathon planning sessions. Seated at a dining room table, they both plugged in their laptops and got busy. The action-packed itinerary came together quickly.

This West Coast destination offered pristine landscapes to explore and exciting activities to share. Engaging in outdoor activities like hiking and biking is a natural way to immerse yourself in this area, but a simple hike in the woods would never do – the planners wanted their *GG*s to have life experiences, the stuff that would make for great memories. Our planners booked many surprises for the trip – and held their breath.

> clue box revisited

As tradition dictated, Kathleen and Perry provided a clue box in advance, to help build excitement for our getaway. The planners began what had evolved into a mini scavenger hunt through the strategic dissemination of e-mails and tiny clues each week for all the planned activities. This clue box, without question, was the most elaborate the *GG*s had seen yet.

destination: Vancouver/ Whistler/Victoria

mode of travel: planes, trains and automobiles

weather: gloriously sunny

cruise directors: Perry & Kathleen

vancouver clue box

Container: Large box wrapped in gold paper covered with clue stickers, and capped with a glittery silver princess tiara

Clues:	Venue:
Tea cup and saucer	Tea at Buchart Gardens
The Taming of the Shrew book	Bard on the Beach tented venue for Shakespearean play
Picture of a Gondola boat	Gondola ride in Whistler
Toy train	Whistler Mountaineer train to Whistler
Martini glass	Just because
Picture of Katharine Hepburn	Hepburn Suite at hotel
Toy plane	Float plane rides to Whistler and Victoria

For several months before the getaway, the planners provided hints that were designed to suggest two possible destinations: London, England, or Paris, France. In addition to being the setting of many of our previously read books, both cities were on many of our "must-visit" lists. To throw off the hostages, Kathleen and Perry teased us with a litany of false clues right up until departure day.

> day 1

On the day of our departure, in a pretty garden, the hostages were met with a fully laden "tea table," complete with Grandma's china service. Atop the outdoor table, the all-important clue box and six traveling Where's Waldo figurines sporting backpacks awaited curious inspection. Backpacks were the only luggage requirement the planners made of the hostages this time. London Fog, a tea beverage created and served almost exclusively in Vancouver by a popular local coffee chain, was prepared and served. A good Vancouver clue, but the name of the drink kept the London, England, possibility in play.

As speculation continued and excitement mounted, the hostages were summoned to the waiting limo and told to climb aboard and listen for clues. While eating our traveling breakfast of pigs in a blanket and English tea scones (again, more false clues), the hostages continued the guessing while dipping into the large clue box. In the background, the *GG* Getaway Travel Tunes played, packed with clues, but no one was listening closely enough. Even when we arrived at the airport, and had settled in to puzzle over the brightly fluorescent lunch bags the planners handed out, we were none the wiser. The destination was still under wraps.

day 1 | planned itinerary

8:00 a.m.	arrive at meeting point
8:30 a.m.	depart in limo
11:30 a.m.	arrive at Toronto Pearson International Airport
1:30 p.m.	depart for Vancouver
3:30 p.m.	arrive in Vancouver
4:30 p.m.	check in to Rosellen Suites
6:00 p.m.	bevies at home base
7:00 p.m.	dinner options: Thai Chili House or Banana Leaf

YES > Dinner at Thai Chili House

> are we there yet?

The pace of our traveling band was reminiscent of the hit TV show *The Amazing Race*, complete with obstacles and frantic behavior. To the great surprise of all, our planners were able to register the girls for their flight and clear security without divulging the final destination to the waiting hostages. Even the airport staff found this travel concept intriguing and helped to maintain the secret. The charade continued with us sitting patiently at an incorrect boarding gate. Then, at boarding time, the gig was up. We were guided to the Vancouver gate. London and Paris would have to wait for another getaway.

We all settled in after take-off; adjusting seats and choosing a movie channel. There was only one thing left to do. As the beverage cart passed by, the travelers looked anxious – how would they be able to pay for a beverage when all of our expenses are taken care of by the planners? "Relax ladies, look in your lunch bag," Perry said. Inside was the "bevie allowance," a $5 bill paper-clipped to a postcard displaying a plane with a cocktail on the tray table. Now that we had opened our lunch bags, it was time to explore their contents. Our favorite Mufflata sandwich,

see recipe in Chapter 7, "*GG* Bites," made an encore appearance from our Toronto getaway, accompanied by honey roasted nuts, a banana, some cookies, a chocolate bar and a package of mints. What's more, we were set up with the tools for all possible traveler's eventualities: wet wipes, hand sanitizer, Dora the Explorer Kleenex, fun straws, Waldo, diva eye covers, ear plugs and neck holders (for Perry naps).

As the plane touched down, the exhilaration started to soar. We had made it to the other side of the country and were ready to take the West by storm. We had grabbed our bags and made our way to ground transportation when a striking woman in a sharp navy suit approached the group and asked "Are you the Giller Girls?" Perry responded quickly, "We are."

› right this way, please

We were ushered into an awaiting vehicle. It was a very long, very white, very new limo. Now even Kathleen gave Perry a surprise glance but it was met with a huge smile. Perry had planned a surprise for everyone, including Kathleen. We were about to embark on a champagne tour of the city and its infamous Stanley Park as a welcome gift from Perry's father, himself a local Vancouverite.

gg discovery

A penthouse suite may seem extravagant, but for large numbers it can actually be cost-efficient. See rosellensuites.com for availability.
· · · · · · · · · ·

› home base

An hour later, we were pulling up in front of the Rosellen Suites apartments. "Where are we? There's no hotel here," we exclaimed, confused. Minutes later, we were walking into our home base suite to the sounds of jazz superstar Diana Krall while a gentle breeze from the open balcony doors, which overlooked a glorious view of the Vancouver skyline and Stanley Park, greeted us. In the meantime, on the suite's rooftop patio was a lavish spread of chilled wines, several varieties of sparkling water, platters of fruit and cheese, and dips and crisps, all flanked by spectacular flowers in tall, clear glass vessels. This magnificent welcome was prepared by the planners' secret ground crew, the *GG* daughters, Ashley and Meg.

As we've noted before, our getaway lodging needn't be a five-star hotel room, so long as it includes a space with a common area large enough to accommodate our end-of-day reminiscences. Perry had secured an entire penthouse apartment with a panoramic view of the city on a beautifully tree-lined street in the heart of Vancouver, minutes from some of the city's best restaurants and Stanley Park.

The penthouse was named the Katharine Hepburn Suite. This apartment was her home base when she visited the city during the 1960s. Although many major cities offer apartments for rent on a weekly basis, few have the charm that this one does.

> day 2

Who doesn't love a picnic on the beach? But how did a picnic hamper magically appear on one of the logs on the shoreline of English Bay? With the help of one of the ground crew, of course. Perry's daughter Ashley had not only prepared a lovely breakfast picnic, but she also provided us with clues to reach the bay from Starbucks where we picked up coffee. She even managed to take secret photos of us as we arrived.

In the afternoon we strolled along False Creek, catching the too-cute water taxi to Granville Island. For a

day 2 | planned itinerary

8:30 a.m. coffee at Starbucks
9:00 a.m. surprise breakfast picnic at English Bay
10:00 a.m. walk and shop on Robson Street
12:00 p.m. lunch at the Wedgewood
2:00 p.m. leave for Granville Island
3:00 p.m. shopping on the island
4:00 p.m. private tour of Granville Island
6:00 p.m. cocktails at Sandbar
7:00 p.m. dinner with Eric and his Edible BC team
10:30 p.m. catch last ferry back to home base

> NO to lunch at Wedgewood (not hungry after a big breakfast)

couple of hours we lazily explored and shopped on the island. Our private guide, Chef Eric, took us on a tour of the Public Market, where he introduced us to the many vendors and culinary experiences in this renowned market. We sampled exotic, custom-blended teas; savored candied salmon (a local delicacy); and tasted authentic baguettes, prepared by the oldest French bakery on the island.

Dinner, which followed early-evening cocktails at a waterfront lounge, turned out to be a participatory affair. We were among a group of 15 people who had signed up for a Cooking with BC's Best Dinner event. A long table decked out in black linen and china was set up in one of the aisles of the market between vendors, a huge transformation from earlier that day when it was a challenge to navigate through the marketplace. We all watched and learned as Chef Eric and his assistant prepared a fabulous six-course meal using the simplest of local ingredients. Yes, the same Chef Eric that had guided us on our delightful afternoon tour of B.C.'s culinary mecca – Granville Island Public Market. What a fabulous end to a great day.

Since food tastes even better with wine, Eric and his Edible BC team cracked open some bottles of British Columbia's best vintages to further enhance the flavors of this truly memorable menu. As the scant remnants of a dessert of iced wine gelatin with fresh berries was cleared away, we realized our tantalizing day of great sights and tastes was coming to an end and, in true Cinderella fashion, we hurried to catch our water taxi at the dock.

> day 3

The Shoe Itinerary never revealed much of the plans for the day ahead, and this day was no exception. It sounded like a busy day! That could mean anything. A 6 a.m.-wake-up call, prompted more queries about the activities that awaited us.

> our chariot

Before we even had the chance to get the coffeepot brewing, the planners announced our departure. But we were appeased en route to our early-morning destination with a stop for a steaming cup of coffee along the way.

While we sipped our brews and wondered about the day's events, a bus pulled up. The surprise was over, or was it? It was the Whistler Mountaineer bus, with a full description of our next destination proudly displayed on its side. It would be taking us to the train terminal, where we would be boarding a privately owned train for an incredibly unique view of the British Columbia terrain. For the next three hours, we rolled along through back-country panoramas from Vancouver to Whistler, whose inaccessibility by car made it only available to passengers on the Whistler Mountaineer. The well-appointed club cars with white linen and uniformed attendants were reminiscent of bygone days of luxury rail travel.

The breakfast we were served included divine omelettes, perfectly prepared toast, and an elaborate coffee and tea service, complete with silver serving pieces. Freshly squeezed orange juice mixed into our mimosas topped off the early-morning meal. The open-air observation car brought the forest close enough to smell the pine trees. Even the noisy train wheels couldn't stifle the sound of the waterfalls crashing against the rocks. Following the shores of Howe Sound, we climbed almost 2,000 feet through the coastal mountains,

day 3 | planned itinerary

6:00 a.m.	wake-up, skip breakfast
7:45 a.m.	walk to the bus pickup
8:15 a.m.	board Whistler Mountaineer
11:30 a.m.	arrive in Whistler
12:00 p.m.	board Whistler gondola
1:00 p.m.	lunch with Jeff on glacier
5:30 p.m.	float plane return to Vancouver
7:00 p.m.	bevies at home base
8:00 p.m.	dinner at Cardero's

> NO to dinner at Cardero's (totally exhausted)

traveling over a trestle bridge high above the roaring rapids below. These sights and sounds delighted even the planners.

Once we reached the village of Whistler, speculation mounted over our next activity. The prospect of whitewater rafting or zip-trekking had some girls seriously asking about alternative activities, such as shopping or lounging in a café. But after a tour of the village, Perry and Kathleen quashed the notion of a fearful adventure by approaching the ticket booth to purchase passage for six on a gondola ride to the top of the mountain.

Boarding a gondola in record-high temperatures of 35 degrees C (95 degrees F) was a new experience for all, even the seasoned skiers among us who were accustomed to riding in much colder weather bundled in many layers. We walked from the gondola station, a short but steep jaunt past 12-foot snowdrifts, to the chairlift. Here, they were handing out blankets for the ride to the top of Whistler Mountain, in spite of the shorts and sandals we all sported. Our group made the ascent, trusting that the planners had made provisions for such a heat-drenched day. If only the hostages knew what surprise was in store for them.

Before long, the summit of Whistler Mountain came into full view and the site of an enormous inukshuk (the symbol for the Vancouver 2010 Olympics) stood atop the mountain. It's believed that these man-made figures may have been used by the Inuit and other Natives for navigation, as a point of reference, or as a marker for hunting grounds or as a food cache. The beacon was positioned in a way to say "we've been here before and we'll show you the way." But even the best-laid plans can be derailed.

gg discovery

A mother often reaps the rewards of her teachings. On this trip, our children proved that they could rally to our cause and demonstrate true GG planning ingenuity.

· · · · · · · · · ·

› planning dilemma

For weeks before our departure, Kathleen and Perry had been finalizing plans with Pat's son Jeff, who lived in Whistler, to provide our lunch high atop the mountain. He was delighted with the idea of surprising his mom's GGs with such a treat.

Unsure of the exact picnic location, Perry started to hike in several directions. She finally spotted a blanket laid out neatly on the glacier, high above her head. She had to coax her *GGs* to walk up a 45-degree hill. But it was worth it. There was a spread of fresh fruit, chilled wine and delicious gourmet paninis. While the rest of us shrieked with excitement, Pat shed a few tears, the proud mother of her son. It was a once-in-a-lifetime memory.

> snow angels, anyone?

Broad smiles and hugs, record-breaking temperatures and fantastic food were the perfect combination for a spectacular day. As we enjoyed our picnic, a hostage *GG* challenged the group: "Who wants to make snow angels in July?"

We left Vancouver that morning dressed in summer togs, but that didn't stop any of us from taking the bait. We all jumped off the blanket and fell on our backs into the snow. It was a scene our families back home would have never believed.

> what's for dinner?

Our planners had created a schedule that matched the precision of a marching band. Once we descended from the glacier, we had exactly one-and-a-half hours to return to Vancouver, change and dash for a cab. When the *GGs* expected a train station, they encountered a lake and a float plane. But there was one more surprise for the day. The spectacular trip back to Vancouver was via a six seater float plane, soaring over the Whistler and Blackcomb Mountains, over yet more glaciers and the landmark Black Tusk Peak. Native people believed the peak was the "seat of thunder" where the legendary thunderbird lived. The rock was said to have been burned by lightning. The group grew very weary during the flight, as the day's many activities and heat took its toll. The planners worried we wouldn't make our dinner reservations.

day 4 | planned itinerary

9:00 a.m.   leisurely breakfast at home base
10:30 a.m.   bike ride in Stanley Park
12:30 p.m.   picnic lunch
2:30 p.m.   relax with bevies
5:30 p.m.   dinner at Vij's
8:00 p.m.   Bard on Beach Theatre

day 5 | planned itinerary

6:45 a.m.   another early rise
8:30 a.m.   float plane to Victoria
10:00 a.m.   whale-watching
2:00 p.m.   bus to Butchart Gardens
2:45 p.m.   afternoon tea – Rose Gardens
7:00 p.m.   float plane to Vancouver
8:30 p.m.   dinner at Chapino's

> to vote or not to vote

It had been a fabulously fun, but tiring day. Once we arrived at our Hepburn suite, we collapsed on our balcony and enjoyed the clear blue vista of the Vancouver skyline. We never did get our second wind and voted unanimously to enjoy the night in our quarters.

> day 4

Even a simple bike ride had our signature GG style stamped on it. On day 4, our ground crew had organized a leisurely bike ride through the city's renowned Stanley Park. But we don't know who was more surprised, the planners or the hostages, to see the bright pink bikes decorated in pink leis awaiting us.

Still, even biking in style couldn't help us with our unpredicted challenge. What was supposed to be a relaxing hour or two bike ride through Stanley Park turned into an extended ordeal because of the way the park had been devastated the previous winter by a wind storm that had uprooted huge, century-old trees. Blocked pathways made the planned route impassible. Parts of this ancient forest had fallen, forcing detours that took us deep into the forest, winding uphill at times through lush growth. Aside from the exhaustion, we were in awe to see the magnitude of the devastation.

The detours had taken us way past lunchtime, and we needed to regroup and reorganize our itinerary during a much-needed rest by an enormous fallen Douglas fir. Our determined planners rallied the group to push on toward their finish, where we could raise a toast to our Olympic feat at a nearby restaurant.

> day 5

We were scheduled to take another float plane ride – this time to the provincial capital, Victoria, on Vancouver Island. As we disembarked the plane we were thrilled by the sight of the Empress Hotel, renowned for its formal English tea service. But tea at the Empress would have been too obvious a choice for our planners.

> whale of a time

A more exciting adventure awaited us, whale-watching! The Gulf Islands are the playground for many family pods of orcas, known as killer whales. In spite of the less-than-glamorous, waterproof, one-size-fits-nobody suit each passenger had to wear on the boat, we were thrilled with the prospect of witnessing these imposing creatures in their natural habitat.

After a windy, bumpy, splash-filled pursuit in our inflatable Zodiac boat, we were rewarded with the sight of majestic leaps and tail-slapping from the whales.

We would see more of nature's splendor at our next stop – a leisurely stroll through Butchart Gardens, one of Canada's most beautiful botanical gardens. Designed by the wife of a concrete baron, the space was once a depleted gravel pit. Now a National Historic Site of Canada, the Butchart Gardens offers 55 acres of wonderful floral displays with more than one million bedding plants in some 700 varieties that bloom from March through October. It was the perfect backdrop for our high tea in the conservatory. Pass the scones, please!

day 6 | planned itinerary

9:30 a.m.   breakfast at Elbow Room

10:30 a.m.   leisurely shopping

2:30 p.m.   Vancouver Art Gallery

5:00 p.m.   refresh at home base

8:00 p.m.   dinner at Tojo's

11:00 p.m.   cocktails at Delilah's Martini Bar

12:30 a.m.   back to home base

> champagne, anyone?

As if there hadn't been enough surprises for the day, our next event was a surprise for us all, including the planners. As we waited for our float plane in Victoria's inner harbor, an attendant began to serve us champagne and chocolate-covered strawberries the size of small peaches. Wow, they really do it right in Victoria!

We should have known – this fabulous treat came compliments of a fellow *GG* who was unable to travel with us. She had arranged for her daughter, a busy doctor living on the island, to deliver the booty and enlist the help of the airline personnel. In the tray was a small pale envelope, which Perry opened and read aloud. "Wish I was with you today. I'm there in spirit! Love, your *GG* sister."

> day 6

By day 6, we were tired, oh so tired. After a late breakfast at the iconic Elbow Room, we wandered downtown and split up to do a bit of our own retail therapy. We were to meet at the Vancouver Art Gallery later that afternoon for a private tour. A highlight was viewing the works by the quintessential Canadian artist Emily Carr, whose art was influenced by the landscape and First Nations cultures of British Columbia and Alaska. After days of enjoying the majestic B.C. scenery, the *GG*s felt a personal connection with Carr's work.

Back at our home base, we gathered for our last cocktail hour on the balcony deck and engaged in our last clothing exchange in preparation for our grand finale dinner. Stilettos for sure. Ashley and Meg, our Vancouver ground crew, joined us for dinner at Tojo's Japanese restaurant. We toasted them for all their assistance and honored them with their very own *GG* Bling bracelets to match the ones we received earlier in the trip.

> the final day

As the *GGs* were finally released from the planners'
blueprint, the fatigue from the weeklong adventures
gave way to mild disappointment. We had laughed and
we had cried with exhaustion. And now we had to pack
and begin our journey back home.

> switching places

On a Saturday morning a couple of months later, our planners became
hostages! As they responded to the sound of the doorbell, both Kathleen
and Perry were met by fellow *GGs* at their respective homes, blindfolded
and whisked off to waiting vehicles.

The cars came to a stop and the blindfolds were removed to reveal
the home of a fellow *GG*. Soon all the traveling *GGs* emerged shouting,
"Surprise! Breakfast is ready!" The newly minted hostages surrendered
their feeble attempts to decipher this mystery. They took their place
around the table to enjoy breakfast, before pausing to unwrap their
recognition gifts – memory photo albums of our Vancouver getaway.

POST CARD

CANADA
1 CENT 1

> *vancouver
post script:*
The planners had wanted
to share with the GGs their
love of the West Coast and
all it had to offer. By the
end of the trip, they
realized that in their great
enthusiasm not to miss

anything, they had
overloaded the itinerary.
Sometimes just having the
time to relax and enjoy each
other's company is enough.
Lesson learned.

MESSAGE

ADDRESS

bite | bite | noun

1. > a light meal of food to
      satisfy appetite
2. > a *GG* nutritional morsel
      offered at any time when
      entertaining, produced
      with creative talent and
      minimal effort

bevie | bev.ee | noun

1. > a liquid specifically
      prepared for human
      consumption
2. > a *GG* libation, with or
      without spirits, that
      facilitates conversation
      when reviewing the previous
      month's book club read

bites & bevies

We believe that the true meaning of hospitality is generosity and warmth, with a little *GG* fun thrown in for good measure. The simplicity of our early meetings has evolved into so much more.

themed nights

Our meetings are often planned around book-inspired themes. It's a wonderful way to create an atmosphere about the book you've selected and turn an ordinary book club night into something special.

tuscany at home | Recreate the warmth of a Tuscan sunset with the clinking of wine glasses and the breaking of bread. Salute!

inspiration

Under the Tuscan Sun
Frances Mayes

Without Reservations
Alice Steinbach

Eat, Pray, Love
Elizabeth Gilbert

Angels & Demons
Dan Brown

"As I held the book in my hands I could see the Tuscan hills and smell the lavender in the air. With the limited time I had on a weeknight, how was I going to bring these emotions to my girls?" —*Kathleen*

> setting the mood

The spirit of this themed meeting leaped off the pages of more than one of our books. The theme was an opportunity to enjoy all things Tuscan, as if to live la bella vita. Our evening was reminiscent of a simpler, rustic time when food, wine and good company were all that mattered. If you can arrange deli meats and cheeses on a platter, boil a few potatoes and scoop ice cream, you'll have a fabulous meal for a perfect evening. Buon appetito!

wine served
Pinot Grigio
(white) and
Chianti Classico
(red)

" If God had intended us to follow recipes he wouldn't have given us grandmothers." —*Linda Henley*

> book club night: *Under the Tuscan Sun*

The theme was especially fitting for Kathleen, our host that night. Italian food has held a special place in her heart ever since she learned to make some authentic, multi-generational recipes from a wonderful Italian friend whom she fondly called Nonna Rocca. On one occasion, Nonna taught her to gently break an egg into a small flour well and work with the mound of fresh pasta – a hands-on experience that captured the pure essence of country cooking. Memories of afternoons spent creating basic, pastoral dishes that burst with flavor was the inspiration for Kathleen's menu for that night.

What was best about the menu Kathleen created for our night is the ease with which she pulled it together. A quick trip to her local Italian bakery and deli (almost every city has one) turned up most of the ingredients in her antipasti platter. Along the way, she picked up an Italian-language newspaper, perfect for wrapping her book selection, parcel style with red string. After assembling her dishes, she only had to organize the music and set the table.

To create the quintessential red-and-white linen tablecloth, Kathleen used classic checkered tea towels, the kind your mother might have had, and layered them in the center of the table to form a runner. On it, she placed tall water glasses of breadsticks, and then book-ended the table with peasant-style platters of antipasti. All this tableau required was the finishing touch of a candle or two.

Next was the music. Kathleen wanted some of it to be traditional, to hold to the evening's theme. Sorting through her collection of music titles, she found a CD of accordion music purchased years ago while on a trip to Italy. Who knew it would find new life as this evening's theme! Other choices included more contemporary artists like Il Divo and Andrea Bocelli. Music would greet the *GG*s as they walked through the door. The stage was set.

There were other moments that made the evening particularly special. Perry and Pat had just returned from a trip to Europe where they visited many of the destinations described in *Without Reservations: The Travels of an Independent Woman* by Alice Steinbach, one of the books we had

> "If we collectively didn't know any better, we'd swear we were in a small Italian café about to sit down to an evening of delightful Italian food. It felt so authentic, right down to the small details."
>
> —GG member

reviewed months earlier. As the girls traced Steinbach's steps, they earmarked their travels with pictures of themselves in the very same locations. Later, the travelers presented each *GG* with a small album of the photographs. "We feel as though we were right there with you!" said one of the *GG* sisters, summarizing exactly what we were all thinking.

Of course, a club meeting night is never complete without a discussion of the book. On the agenda this night was also an opportunity to highlight the independent spirit of another woman following her dreams – the main character of *Under the Tuscan Sun*, a book that was top-rated by the group. **See the *GG* Book List in Chapter 2, "On the Bookshelf."** Following our exchange was the usual tug at our travel heart by Perry. "So, what do you think, girls? Should we do the Chianti trail in Tuscany, *GG* style? Since we all loved the book, wouldn't you think we'd love the region, too?" As each *GG* lamented about this prospect we were reminded of our future possibilities.

Months later, we also received tiny colorful hand-painted cream pitchers from another member, traveling without her *GG* sisters. She, too, had followed a book character's path and visited the house that had inspired author Frances Mayes to write *Under the Tuscan Sun*. Naturally, we were touched by these gestures. Not only do they connect us to the books we've read, but they also highlight and strengthen the bond between us.

> tricks & tips

You don't need an Italian mentor to prepare this classically perfect alfresco show of hospitality. Simple and pure flavors set the tone for any day or night in Tuscany. Here are some quick and easy suggestions for creating your own Tuscany at Home evening:

florist or nursery. Select bright florals that work with your napkins and serving pieces.

> Pick napkins in a variety of colors. There's no need to match. Primary colors look great beside Mediterranean food and drinks.

> Abandon the stemware and use short, clear juice glasses for your wine selections for a genuine vineyard feel.

> Package books parcel style: use Italian-language newspaper to wrap and red string to tie it together.

> If you're lucky enough to have a large wooden table, leave it uncovered for a rustic feel. If not, choose a simple linen tablecloth in white as your canvas for the night. Vintage tea towels work perfectly as table runners.

> Use multicolored platters and dishes. Mustard yellows, rusty reds and oranges, olive greens and aqua blues work particularly well.

> Fill a couple of tall glasses with breadsticks to accent the table beautifully.

> Choose fresh-picked flowers (sunflowers are perfect) from your garden, your local

› menu

Playing off the hospitality of rustic European entertaining, the casual and communal format of this menu blends friendship with laughter perfectly. See recipes in Chapter 7, *"GG Bites"* and Chapter 8, *"GG Bevies."*

bevie match-ups

booktini
lemon drop

·

wine
**Pinot Grigio
Chianti Classico**

menu

starter
antipasti platter

·

soup
stracciatella

·

salad
potinis

·

dessert
designer ice-cream sandwiches

playlist

Anything from Italian folk music to operatic pop ballads will do

·

Verdi, Romanza
by Andrea Bocelli

·

e2
by Eros Ramazzotti

·

Ancora by Il Divo

"The trouble with eating Italian food is that five or six days later, you're hungry again." —*George Miller*

casual cottage

casual cottage | An hour's drive from home but miles from everyday life, the *GGs* gave new meaning to the camping experience.

inspiration

The Hatbox Letters
Beth Powning

Confessions of a Shopaholic
Sophie Kinsella

Crow Lake
Mary Lawson

Divine Secrets of the Ya-Ya Sisterhood
Rebecca Wells

" Happiness is a bowl of cherries and a book of poetry under a shade tree." —*Astrid Alauda*

› setting the mood

Who could resist the temptation of an afternoon book club meeting,
picnic style, in the company of a summer breeze? Along the shores of Lake
Huron, the tiny village of Grand Bend provided the GGs the perfect venue
for an overnight mid-week getaway. It was a welcomed departure from
our typical book club meeting format. The menu for this special themed
meeting reflects the unique twists of a country road, filled with surprises
around every corner.

wine served
Chardonnay (white) and
Pinot Noir (red)

> book club night: *The Hatbox Letters*

Near the end of summer, Kathleen rented a cottage 30 minutes outside of London, Ontario, for a mid-week sleepover or, as we lovingly referred to it, *GG* camp. How could any of us resist such an offer? It was a glorious

summer day and the opportunity to spend it out of doors with our nearest and dearest was appealing in the extreme.

The *GGs* love to travel in style, and this occasion was no exception. One of our beloved *GGs* owns a convertible, so with the weather in our favor, we hopped into the car (roof down, of course) and headed for the cottage. We're always looking for opportunities to pull out our favorite *GG* gems from our getaways, so we donned our pearls and wrapped our belly-dancing scarves (from the Pelee Island getaway) around our heads, Audrey Hepburn style. We completed the look with the biggest sunglasses we could find.

Off we went! As we entered the cottage, we noticed a giant hatbox. Inside, our books awaited, wrapped in white paper to look like envelopes, complete with address and stamp. Official camp mail. There have been times when some *GGs* have been unable to join us on our getaways, but Kathleen came up with the perfect solution on this outing: we would record our adventures in a journal. It would give us all an opportunity to note personal reactions and emotions and share them with everyone.

With her days at summer camp top of mind, Kathleen sought to recapture the experience for her *GGs* on this getaway. She had set up a craft table where the *GGs* would be making their own bracelets – not the woven plastic strips she labored over as a camper, but brilliantly embellished trinkets boasting lots of *GG* bling. The beads, neatly arranged in clear containers and sparkling in the sunlight with promise, proved the building blocks for the perfect memento of our camping experience.

Kathleen faced a unique challenge when it came to feeding the group. Like many vacation properties, kitchen amenities at this cottage were more about necessity than gourmet. So she kept our dinner simple and delicious with the emphasis on simple. In keeping with the cottage theme, she focused on taking advantage of the barbecue and surprised us with her own special grilled pizza and grilled Caesar salad. The *GGs* are never shy about bringing out their personal favorites, and for this occasion Perry offered to provide her famous tropical gazpacho. Topping it off with multiple summer desserts, what could be easier? **See recipes in Chapter 7, "GG Bites."**

Kathleen had already assembled pizza toppings, purchased a pre-made pizza crust, prepared a head of romaine lettuce, washed a bowl of fresh berries and sliced up a large watermelon in the tiny kitchen area. But there was a twist: we would all be pitching in to make our own pizzas.

As the sun slid down from the clear blue sky leaving streaks of orange dancing on the horizon, the craft table was quickly cleared for al fresco dining. The cocktails were mixed, the barbecue lit and the fun encouraged. After we devoured the last morsel of pizza and dessert, we kicked up our feet and reminisced of other lazy summer days.

P.S. It's still unclear what came first as the GGs arrived at their destination that day: the sound of tires on gravel or of gleeful laughter in the air? With windswept hair and anticipation, we were ready to make the most of a mid-week sleepover.

> tricks & tips

Sharing a sunset with friends is the quintessential summertime must-do. Here are some quick and easy suggestions for creating your own casual cottage day:

> To create tiny individual lanterns, place votive candles in small jelly jars, encircle the rims with crafter's wire and twist the loose ends to form long hooks. Hook each jar to the back of your guests' chairs. Another option is to hang the jars from tree branches or a patio umbrella.

> Use a tablecloth in citrus shades or beach motifs for a casual cottage style. Purchase a few yards of striped canvas (resembling an awning) from a fabric store to create a runner down the center of the table. Consider pinking shears to cut the brightly colored fabric into individual rectangular pieces for placements.

> For an instant surprise of color, use a new, brightly hued bedsheet as a tablecloth. Let your food be the centerpiece.

> Use a sand pail as a whimsical ice bucket. Placed at one end of the table, it announces a 'help-yourself' casual attitude.

> Use small climbing branches (wisteria and honeysuckle work great) down the center of the table and tuck in seed packages between the leaves for a kitschy floral arrangement.

> Scatter small piles of beach sand and seashells on the table to bring in some beach fun.

> Clip large foliage, such as hosta leaves, from your garden to use as placemats, and smaller leaves for coasters.

> Break out the patio stemware in a variety of hot colors.

> Have fun with your serving utensils. For example, use kids' colorful sand tools as salad servers.

> Plug in lively summertime music – anything from The Beach Boys to Backstreet Boys.

> menu

Start with simple store-bought dips and a variety of crudités while you work on the pizza. Enjoy all the simple fresh flavors of the season as you select your menu. *See recipes in Chapter 7, "GG Bites."*

bevie match-ups

booktini

fruit *GG* on ice

•

wine

Chardonnay
Pinot Noir

menu

soup

tropical gazpacho

•

salad 'n' stuff

grilled Caesar salad
grilled pizza

•

dessert

berry bowl
designer ice-cream
sandwiches

playlist

You'll want
music that's light
and fun.

•

Beach Boys

•

Sheryl Crow

•

Nellie Furtado

•

Bryan Adams

asian delight

asian delight | Bridging the divide between the GGs and this ancient culture.

inspiration

The Good Earth
Pearl S. Buck

The Bonesetter's Daughter
Amy Tan

The Time In Between
David Bergen

Mao's Last Dancer
Li Cunxin

❝ Nothing would be more tiresome than eating and drinking if God had not made them a pleasure as well as a necessity." —*Voltaire*

› setting the mood

We love this theme so much we've used it more than once. It's true that we "eat with our eyes," and we don't think many other food cultures exemplify this sentiment better than Asian cuisine. The flavors and colors instantly take us from our everyday life to an exotic destination. The menu for this evening included a blaze of color, with a variety of salads. The ingredients look lengthy and complicated, but these dishes come together quickly.

As we joined the book's characters on their travels, we were struck by their dedication and sacrifice to keep their culture and traditions alive.

wine served
Riesling (white) and
Beaujolais (red)

› book club night: *The Good Earth*

Perry selected the book *The Good Earth* and decided to have an afternoon meeting. This allowed the *GG*s to enjoy the warm summer weather and the view of the lake from her patio. Fantastic!

The importance of family and tradition, which was a running theme throughout the book, made this book selection a natural choice for one of our most treasured events in *GG* history. We were expecting our first baby! What a perfect opportunity and venue to plan a surprise baby shower for our *GG* mom-to-be. Imagine her surprise as she rounded the corner of the house to find balloons, decorations and a group of anxiously awaiting *GG*s.

But, first you'll need to understand some history of how we got to this date. A few months before, at a regular *GG* book club meeting, one of our members presented each *GG* with a small gift bag. First, there was a rattle, then safety pins and, finally, booties. Kathleen got there first. "Are we having a baby?" she asked our *GG* host. The resounding "yes" from the expectant mom was followed by tears, laughter and hugs of congratulations.

Over the next few months, we began planning our surprise *GG* baby shower. Perry chose an Asian theme to play off her book selection, which celebrates a culture steeped in family traditions. Instead of plates, our lunch was served in Bento boxes, reminiscent of our first *GG* getaway in Toronto when our *GG* mom-to-be had delighted over this style of presentation. Perry went to great lengths in the Chinatown district to find these boxes. Hours of wrong turns, language barriers and frustration were well worth the extra effort for this very special occasion. She prepared a replica of that lunch in an effort to make this day truly memorable for the expectant mom.

Of course, the event also called for a special baby shower gift. In keeping with our book club roots, we decided to each purchase one of our most treasured children's books; **see sidebar, right.** We went through bookshelves, looked under beds and questioned unsuspecting older children, all in search of our family favorites. It was an opportunity for many of us to recall fond memories of bedtime stories. Our new baby would have an instant library of very special, much-loved books, personally autographed by the *GG*s.

For an added touch, the *GG*s sourced a wall hanging by a local artist depicting an expectant mother. As for the decor, the table was set with shining glass bowls bursting with colorful, exotic dragon fruit. A striking gold table runner threaded its way down the table, deflecting the sunshine onto the crystal and silver. The cheerful balloons tied to our chairs danced in the gentle breeze that came off the nearby lake.

Strains of *Buddha-Bar V* floated in the air as we leisurely enjoyed our lunch. On that beautiful summer day, our guest of honor got busy unwrapping the baby gifts that we had so lovingly chosen. But we knew the best gift of all would be the arrival of this tiny new life.

books for GG baby library

- The Busy Little Train Anna Claybourne
- Baby's First Colors Hinkler Books
- On the Night You Were Born Nancy Tillman
- Llama Llama Mad at Mama Anna Dewdney
- Cars and Trucks and Things That Go Richard Scarry
- My Little Animal Book Roger Priddy
- The Runaway Bunny Margaret Wise Brown
- Russell the Sheep Rob Scotton
- Mama's Right Here Liza Baker
- The Little Prince Antoine de Saint-Exupéry

› tricks & tips

Less is more when it comes to this theme. We love to decorate the table by using fruits and vegetables, providing texture and intense colors. Here are some suggestions for creating your own Asian Delight day:

› Submerge colorful fruit in the bottom of a clear glass vase and add floating candles.

› For a simple centerpiece, bundle several stalks of bamboo with colorful ribbon and place in a slim, clear container. Or place simple stems of fresh ginger flowers with bear grass in two or more small clear glass containers.

› Wrap chopsticks with a band of origami paper for a colorful touch on each plate.

› Fill several Chinese takeout containers with small drinking glasses, slightly shorter than the top of the boxes. Fill each glass with brightly colored gerber daisies.

› Use white china for a fabulous backdrop, so brightly colored decorations will pop off the table.

› Scatter fortune cookies down the center of the table or secure one to each napkin with a red ribbon around the center of the cookie.

› Add instant Asian tradition with red linen or paper napkins.

› If you're having trouble finding Oriental music, choose soft string selections, such as those from Vivaldi.

› For exotic centerpieces, fill a clear glass vase of any shape with Vietnamese dragon fruit and lychee nuts. Add super impact by skewering lychees into the dragon fruit with small wooden skewers or toothpicks to create a 'bouquet.'

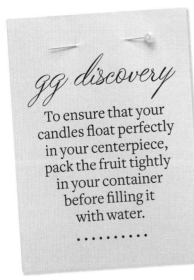

gg discovery

To ensure that your candles float perfectly in your centerpiece, pack the fruit tightly in your container before filling it with water.

· · · · · · · · · ·

> menu

The color and texture of this food make a lasting impression. It's a little more work to prepare this menu than others, but if you've got the time, it's well worth the effort. See recipes in Chapter 7, "*GG* Bites" and Chapter 8, "*GG* Bevies."

bevie match-ups

booktini
pear-lychee

·

wine
Riesling
Beaujolais

menu

starters
Thai spiced nuts
fresh Vietnamese
spring rolls

·

salads
Asian coleslaw
Asian noodle
& shrimp platter

·

soups & surprises
baked salmon
with lime
ginger mayo

playlist

Some Eastern
music for the
Western ear

·

Buddha-Bar V
by David Visan

·

Jai Jai Jai by Wa

·

The Essence
by Deva Premal

gg bites

The GGs come to the rescue with gourmet tips and step-by-step instructions. Our tested recipes, compiled from more than 60 book club meetings, come complete with a guide rating the degree of difficulty.

starters 158 | soups & surprises 166

salads 174 | desserts 178 | travel food 184

starters | These starters help kick off a fabulously easy evening of entertaining.

Cheats...with little time and effort
Big on flavor, yet little on effort, these easy-to-prepare recipes will make it to the table in minutes.

Almost cheats...in 30 minutes or less
These creative concoctions are the recipes from surprising sources. Still easy to manage with some shortcuts.

Soooo worth the effort
When you have the time and inclination to take things to the next level, you'll want to try these recipes. Your book club sisters will so appreciate them!

thai spiced nuts

PREP: 10 MIN OR LESS | COOK: 30 MIN | FEEDS A BUNCH

So yummy you'd better make extra to store in the freezer! From our Asian Delight menu

1/4	cup liquid honey
4	tsp green curry paste
2	tsp canola oil
3/4	tsp salt
11/4	cups whole almonds
11/2	cups pecan halves
11/2	cups roasted salted cashews
1/3	cup shredded coconut

> Combine honey, curry paste, oil and salt. Add nuts and coconut and mix until completely coated. Spread in a single layer on parchment-lined cookie sheet. Bake in a preheated oven at 300°F for 30 minutes, stirring once after 15 minutes. Nuts should be golden brown. Cool. Makes 4½ cups

tip: Store in an airtight container in a cool place for up to 1 week or freeze up to 1 month.

cream cheese & jelly

PREP: 10 MIN OR LESS | SERVES 8+

Fast, fun and fab

> Slightly warm 1 pkg (8 oz) cream cheese in the microwave on high power for 25 seconds and place on serving plate.

> Top with 2 oz of hot pepper jelly, marmalade or any other preferred jelly. Sprinkle with chopped nuts such as almonds or walnuts.

cheese & fruit tray

PREP: 10 MIN OR LESS | SERVES 8+

Sassy and simple

> Place 3 8-oz chunks of cheese on a very large colorful tray or platter.

> Place martini glass in center and fill with any type of nut. Surround with several varieties of crackers placing them in small groups, alternating with fresh grapes or other fruits (figs, dates), and whole nuts.

saucy salsa dip

PREP: 10 MIN OR LESS | SERVES 8+

You don't have to travel to Mexico to feel the heat

650	ml medium to hot purchased salsa
4	large tomatoes, diced
3	bunches green onions, diced
2 1/2	tsp chopped garlic
1	bunch whole cilantro, chopped and crushed

Juice from 1 lemon
Pinch of salt and pepper

> Combine all ingredients in a bowl and refrigerate for at least 2 hours or up to 24 hours. Makes 3 cups

shrimp dip

PREP: 10 MIN OR LESS | SERVES 8-10

So low in calories it's a guiltless pleasure
Served at our "A" Retro Christmas night

1   cup low-fat dry cottage cheese (drain if using creamy cottage cheese)
1/4   cup freshly squeezed lemon juice
2   green onions, chopped (reserve a 2-inch piece for garnish)
1   small frozen shrimp ring (reserve 3 for garnish)
1   tbsp seafood sauce
1/2   tsp horseradish
Sea salt to taste
Freshly ground tricolor pepper to taste
Dash of Tabasco

> Place all ingredients into the bowl of a food processor. Pulse until well combined, avoiding overprocessing.

Place dip into a bowl that has been lined with plastic wrap. Refrigerate for at least 1 hour or up to 24 hours.

> Unmould the dip by inverting bowl onto a plate and removing the plastic wrap. Garnish with green onion curls (see tip) and reserved shrimp and serve. Circle dip with crackers or pita bread triangles or crudités.

tips: If you're really short on time, scoop the dip into a small bowl and place in the freezer for 15 to 20 minutes.
> Curl green onions by splitting the green tops lengthwise in 4-inch sections and placing in ice water for 1 hour.

artichoke garlic dip

PREP: 10 MIN OR LESS | SERVES 6-8

From pantry to meeting in a flash; a favorite forever.

1/3   cup grated Parmesan cheese
1 1/2 cups mayonnaise (low-fat works well)
1   10-oz can artichoke hearts, drained and finely chopped
3-6   cloves garlic, crushed
1 1/2 cups grated mozzarella

> Mix all ingredients well and place in an ovenproof dish. Let sit in the refrigerator for at least 2 to 3 hours.

> When ready to serve, heat in microwave on high for 60 seconds until cheese starts to melt. Stir and heat again in microwave on high for 60 seconds or until hot throughout.

> Serve with crostini, sliced baguette or crackers.

tip: Use a simple French onion soup dish to serve, perfect for reheating.

goat cheese pie

PREP: 30 MIN OR LESS | SERVES 10-12

The colorful layers make this a show-stopper. Pair it with one of our GG booktinis, we suggest the Jeweled GG James Bond

DRESSING
1   tsp finely chopped fresh thyme
1   tsp finely chopped fresh rosemary
1   clove garlic, finely chopped
2   tbsp balsamic vinegar
1   tbsp extra-virgin olive oil
Salt and pepper to taste

8   oz goat cheese, softened
1/3   cup each: sun-dried tomatoes, black Kalamata olives and green pimento-stuffed olives, finely chopped

> To prepare dressing, combine and mix all ingredients together. Set aside.

> Assemble pie by spreading goat cheese into 1-inch thick circle or square on a plate. Combine tomatoes and olives. Add dressing to tomato-olive mixture, mixing until well coated and spread evenly over cheese. Serve with crostini, sliced baguette or crackers.

tip: Ingredients can be prepared and refrigerated for up to 1 day before serving.

antipasti platter

PREP: 15-20 MIN | SERVES 8-10

The aromas of your neighborhood deli come alive as you do little more than arrange ingredients on a rustic platter. From our Tuscany at Home menu

8-10   oz each: capicola, prosciutto
       and mortadella, thinly sliced
16-20 oz sliced provolone or
       fontina cheese
4   oz each: cured black olives;
       canned marinated eggplants;
       canned marinated
       artichokes; green olives;
       bottled roasted red peppers
2   small flavored loaves of bread
       (i.e., olive and hot pepper)
8-10   oz piece Parmigiano-Reggiano cheese
Extra-virgin olive oil (for dipping)
Balsamic vinegar (for dipping)

tips: There's no need to be neat with this platter. It should look rustic!
> Drain small quantities of pickled/bottled foods by either placing in a colander or a coffee filter fitted over a small bowl. Save the oil or pickling juice for storing any leftovers.

> Arrange deli meats and provolone cheese on the perimeter of a very large platter. Drain canned/bottled items and arrange in small piles in the center of your platter.

> Tear or cut bread into thick chunks or slices, about 1 inch thick. Place breads at either ends of the platter.

> Using a vegetable peeler, shave half of the block of Parmigiano-Reggiano cheese into big curls and scatter all over the plate. Finish with fresh parsley sprigs or some grated lemon rind.

> Serve with decanters of extra-virgin olive oil and the best balsamic vinegar in your pantry for dipping breads.

cutest crudités & dip

PREP: 10 MIN OR LESS | SERVES ONE CONTAINER PER PERSON

Small punches of colour hit the spot

> cute method: Hollow out green, red or yellow peppers and use as containers for any store-bought dip.

> cuter method: Place the store-bought dip (in its original container) into a colorful flower pot that's deep enough to hide the container. Place your veggies in any attractive bowl or serving platter. Remove the dip container lid and, voilà, instant fun.

> cutest method: Spoon 1-2 tbsp of store-bought dip (a variety is a great idea) into the bottom of shot glasses or juice glasses. Place a variety of cut veggies standing upright into the glasses, using the dip to anchor them.

tip: Give your seldom-used liqueur glasses new purpose by filling them with dips and sliced veggies.

fresh vietnamese spring rolls

PREP: 30-40 MIN OR LESS | SERVES 15

These sound difficult but if you can chop the ingredients, they have your name all over them. From our Asian Delight menu

CHILI DIPPING SAUCE

1/3	cup cold water
1	tsp granulated sugar
2	tbsp fish sauce
1	tbsp white vinegar
1	small red chili, finely chopped
1	tbsp chopped fresh coriander leaves

SPRING ROLLS

30	medium cooked shrimp
15	small round rice paper wrappers
1 1/2	cups bean sprouts
1	cup packed, fresh coriander leaves
1/2	cup packed, fresh mint
1	medium carrot, cut into short thin strips
6-8	scallions, cut lengthwise in slivers
1/2	cup finely chopped roasted peanuts (optional)

Grated rind of 2 limes

3-4	oz dried rice vermicelli, soaked in warm water for 20 min. and drained
3	tbsp sweet chili sauce

> To make dipping sauce, place cold water in a small bowl. Add the sugar and stir until dissolved.

> Stir in remaining ingredients. Pour into a small dipping bowl. Set aside.

> Peel and devein shrimp. Dip a rice paper wrapper into lukewarm water until it softens, around 30 seconds, and place it on your work surface. Place 2 shrimp in the center of the wrapper and top with a small handful of bean sprouts, 1 tbsp coriander, ½ tbsp mint, a few carrot and scallion strips, peanuts (if using), ¼ tsp of lime rind, ¼ cup of vermicelli. Top filling with ½ tsp of chili sauce.

> Gently flatten the filling down, fold in two ends and roll up to resemble a parcel. Lay seam-side down in an airtight container and sprinkle with a little water. Cover with plastic wrap. Repeat until 15 spring rolls are completed.

> Makes 15 spring rolls; ½ cup dipping sauce

tip: Use store-bought chili dipping sauce for Vietnamese spring rolls if you don't have time to make your own.

welsh rarebit

PREP: 20 MIN OR LESS | SERVES 8-10 AS A DIP

This Sunday morning family favorite works perfectly as a cheese fondue for friends. Served during our Atonement book night

2	tbsp unsalted butter
2	tbsp all-purpose flour
1	tsp Dijon mustard
1	tsp Worcestershire sauce
1/2	tsp kosher salt
1/2	tsp freshly ground black pepper
1/2	cup porter beer
3/4	cup heavy cream or whole milk
6	oz (approximately 1 1/2 cups) shredded cheddar cheese
2	drops hot sauce
1	large loaf of crusty bread, torn into bite-size pieces, about 6 cups

> In a medium saucepan over low heat, melt butter and whisk in flour constantly for 2 to 3 minutes, being careful not to brown the flour. Whisk in mustard, Worcestershire sauce, salt and black pepper until smooth. Add beer, then cream, whisking until combined.

> Gradually add cheese, stirring constantly, until cheese melts and sauce is smooth; this will take 4 to 5 minutes. Add hot sauce. Pour mixture into fondue pot to keep warm until ready to serve with pieces of bread.

soups & surprises | Make into a meal or serve as a side. A perfect addition to any book club meeting.

stracciatella

PREP: 15 MIN | COOK: 10 MIN | SERVES 4-6 AS A STARTER

This delightful Italian soup is as rich and golden as a Tuscan sunset. From our Tuscany at Home menu

4   cups chicken broth
2   eggs (preferably free range for a deep golden color)
1/2   cup freshly grated Parmesan cheese
Freshly ground white or black pepper to taste
Chopped fresh parsley (optional)

> In a stockpot, bring chicken stock to a boil, and then reduce to simmer. Beat eggs with cheese and add to simmering broth. Place lid on pot. Simmer for 4 to 5 minutes without stirring.

> Remove lid and with a spoon gently test the centre of the egg mixture – it should look like scrambled eggs. Once the egg mixture is set (firm), use a potato masher and mash the egg mixture into little pieces.

> Place soup in small bowls, coffee cups or chunky heat-resistant glasses. Add pepper and sprinkle with a little parsley, if using.

tropical gazpacho à la Perry

PREP: 15-20 MIN | SERVES 10-12

Summer isn't summer without the tang of this quick and delectable favorite. The sweetness of pineapple is the perfect balance for the rich tomato. From our Casual Cottage menu

6   cups tomato juice
1   cup pear juice
2   small mangos, diced
1/2   small pineapple, peeled, cored and diced
1/2   red bell pepper, diced
1/2   yellow, orange or green bell pepper, diced
Juice of 4 limes
4   dashes of hot pepper sauce (or to taste)
3/4   cup chopped fresh cilantro
Salt and pepper to taste
Cilantro sprigs for garnish
1   lime, cut into thin wedges for garnish

> In a large bowl, combine tomato and pear juices. Add the remaining 7 ingredients, season with salt and pepper. Refrigerate for at least 4 hours. For a smoother consistency, pulse with blender until desired consistency.

> To serve, pour into a bowl, garnish with cilantro sprigs and lime wedges.

tip: Serve soup with bread sticks in tall glasses for a whimsical touch.

tetra soup à la GG

PREP: 10 MIN | SERVES 4-6

Simply heat, serve in a bowl and garnish. Voilà!

4   cups butternut squash soup
1/2   oz brandy
3   tsp sour cream
Freshly grated nutmeg

> Transfer soup to a pot. Add brandy and simmer till heated through. Pour evenly into four 6 to 8 oz serving bowls. Spoon sour cream into small Ziploc bag and seal. Snip one corner of the bag and squeeze a small amount of sour cream into the center of the soup. Grate nutmeg or sprinkle tiny amount of ground nutmeg over sour cream as garnish. Serve immediately with bread sticks.

fast 'n' fab french onion soup

🍴🍴 PREP: 15 MIN | COOK: 20-30 MIN
SERVES 4-6, DEPENDING ON SIZE OF RAMEKINS

A well-loved old family favourite

4	cups beef broth or onion soup
1/4	cup dry sherry
1	8-oz can freeze-dried onion rings (reserve some for garnish)

Freshly ground black pepper to taste

4-6	pieces French bread or rusk rounds
8-10	oz grated cheese mix (See "6 Great Ideas," right)

> In a 1-quart pot, place first three ingredients and bring to a boil. Season to taste with black pepper. Set aside. You can prepare this a day before and refrigerate it.

> Cut a French baguette into 1-inch thick slices, about ½ inch smaller than the circumference of ramekin and toast bread on broiler till golden brown. Ladle soup into ramekins, filling them about ⅔ full.

> Top with toast or rusk and sprinkle liberally with cheese. Place in a preheated oven at 375°F and bake for 20 to 30 minutes or until cheese is browned and bubbling. Serve hot from oven, garnished with onion rings.

pesto triangles

🍴 PREP: 10 MIN OR LESS | SERVES 6-8

Spread, toast and serve

2	pesto cubes, thawed (See pesto cubes recipe, right)
2	large pita pockets

> Spread one thawed pesto cube evenly onto one side of pita pocket. Repeat. Cut pockets into small triangles. Place triangles under broiler till slightly browned. Serve with dip.

tip: Don't be afraid to oversprinkle the cheese over the lip of the ramekin. No one ever complains about extra melted cheese on their French onion soup.

6 great ideas
to make these recipe essentials ready in an instant

1 fresh herbs
Place fresh herbs – parsley, sage or dill – in a freezer bag for a perfect quick 10-minute (or less) dip addition. No need to chop them up before using because they'll crumble easily while still frozen.

2 cool whip
For an easy way to decorate a dessert, place frozen Cool

Whip into a freezer bag and store in freezer until ready to use. Thaw slightly and snip one corner of the bag for an instant pastry bag to pipe cakes, muffins, ice cream and other desserts.

3 grated cheese
Several small, leftover pieces of cheese from your meeting can be grated and placed in a freezer bag to make instant hot canapés. Or simply sprinkle cheese on tetra-packaged soup to jazz it up before serving.

4 garlic
Chop fresh garlic or simply peel cloves and pop them into a freezer bag before storing them in the freezer. Garlic is ready when you need it.

5 pesto cubes
To prepare pesto cubes, blend 1/2 cup fresh basil, 1/4 cup pine nuts, along with 2 cloves garlic and 1/3 cup extra-

virgin olive oil until it forms a thick paste. Fill ice cube trays with mixture and freeze. Pop the cubes into a freezer bag and you're ready to create. You can also make roasted red pepper cubes by substituting roasted red pepper for basil.

6 wooden skewers
Soak wooden skewers in water for an hour or two, and then place in a large freezer bag to keep in their moisture until they're ready for a hot grill.

roasted veggie dip

✦ PREP: 10 MIN | SERVES 8+

Nothing could be simpler and tastier

2   cups store-bought hummus
       or cream cheese
1   cup chopped grilled vegetables
1   tsp lemon juice

> Place all ingredients into a food processor and pulse until well chopped but not puréed. Serve with pita or flat bread crisps.

tip: Store leftover grilled veggies into a freezer bag, thaw and add to recipe when you're ready to make it.

pineapple meatballs

✦ PREP: 10 MIN | COOK: 35 MIN | SERVES 8+

These perfectly sweet gems served at our "A" Retro Christmas night

1   1-lb pkg frozen plain meatballs
1/2   cup pineapple chunks, drained
       (reserve liquid)
2   cups canned pineapple juice

> Place frozen meatballs in shallow baking pan. Pour pineapple chunks and juice evenly over meatballs.

> Bake in a preheated oven at 325°F for 35 to 40 minutes or until juice has evaporated to half the volume. Spoon meatballs onto serving dish and top with strained reserved juice.

quiche

✦ PREP: 10 MIN | COOK: 35-40 MIN | SERVES 6-8

No one will ever tell it's not homemade

1   frozen 9" quiche, any variety or size
1/2   cup grated cheese, cheddar, Swiss
       or other variety

> Preheat oven according to package directions. Remove quiche from foil pie plate while frozen and transfer to glass pie plate. Top with cheese and bake accordingly. Cut and serve.

baked salmon with lime ginger mayo

PREP: 30 MIN | COOK: 15-20 MIN
SERVES 8-10

Yummmmm hot or cold, this is a winner. The recipe's simplicity highlights the Asian culture and the chi among the crowd when you serve it. From our Asian Delight menu

LIME GINGER MAYO

1/2	cup low-fat yogurt
1/2	cup light mayonnaise
2	tsp fresh lime juice
2	tsp minced gingerroot
1	tsp minced garlic

BAKED SALMON

1	2-lb salmon fillet
1	bunch fresh dill, divided
3	lemons, sliced thinly, divided

Salt and fresh ground black pepper to taste

GARNISHES

Cherry tomatoes; lime slices (optional)

> In a small bowl, stir together all ingredients for Lime Ginger Mayo. Cover and refrigerate for at least 1 hour.

> Rinse salmon and pat dry with paper towel. Let stand at room temperature for about 30 minutes. Cut a piece of foil large enough to wrap around salmon. Place ⅓ of dill and lemon slices on foil, place salmon on top. Sprinkle with salt and pepper. Cover with another ⅓ of dill and lemon slices. Wrap foil, folding edges to seal. Bake in a preheated oven at 375°F for about 15 to 20 minutes (or until salmon is barely opaque and flakes easily with a fork).

> Remove from foil, place on large platter, garnishing with remaining dill and lemon slices, plus lime and tomatoes, if using. Serve either hot, warm or at room temperature.

grilled pizza

PREP: 25 MIN | COOK: 7-10 MIN | SERVES 4-6

A multitude of hands help turn simple pizza dough into a delicious cottage creation. Prepare the toppings before the crowd arrives and let them pick their own toppings. From our Casual Cottage menu

1-2	frozen or fresh pizza dough, or baked 12″ pizza
1/2	cup extra-virgin olive oil (extra for brushing)
1	small onion, cut into rings
All-purpose flour for rolling dough	
1/4-1/3	cup tomato sauce or basil pesto
5	oz grated mozzarella

TOPPINGS

4	oz grilled chicken, Parma ham or any other protein, sliced (optional)
1/4	cup sliced artichoke hearts, canned or marinated
1/4	cup sliced black or green pitted olives and/or diced green peppers
1/4	cup cooked bacon pieces
1/3	cup feta cheese

> Thaw dough ball in refrigerator overnight. Allow dough to reach room temperature while you prepare toppings.

> Add oil to skillet on medium heat and sauté onions until they soften and are golden brown. Remove from heat and let cool.

> Heat the barbecue to 450°F. Oil the BBQ grill racks.

step 1: If you're using store-bought crust, go to Step 2.

> Flour smooth surface before working with dough ball. Flatten ball with the palm of your hand and stretch as you turn the ball clockwise on the floured surface. Flip the dough over and continue stretching. You could use a rolling pin. Add more flour if dough is sticky. Dough is ready for toppings when it forms an oval and you can pick it up off the surface and pull it slightly. The idea is to be rustic and irregular.

> Place the dough on a floured cutting board. Brush the surface of the dough with extra-virgin olive oil. Invert dough from cutting board onto the grill, placing oil-side-down on grill. Grill for 2 to 3 minutes, watching closely.

> Add oil to face-side-up of crust before removing from grill. Remove baked crust from grill, flipping it again so the oiled side is facing down onto cutting board. Turn the grill down to 350°F.

step 2: Spread tomato sauce onto baked crust. Evenly spread half of the grated mozzarella and evenly disperse the remaining toppings. Top with the remaining cheese. Slide the pizza from the cutting board onto the preheated 450°F grill and close the lid.

> Cook for 3 to 5 minutes more or until cheese is melted. Watch the pizza

closely; the cooking process can be quick depending on your grill. Remove from the grill when the cheese has melted, by sliding onto the cutting board or a wooden pizza paddle. Drizzle with olive oil and cut into small pieces. Serve hot or at room temperature.

> Makes 1 12-inch pizza

tip: Use a small oil-soaked cotton cloth to coat the barbecue grill racks.

salads | A side can easily become a meal. Buy ingredients already packaged or chop to your heart's content.

salad on the run

PREP: 10 MIN | SERVES 6

Fast, fabulous and incredibly easy when you need a quick side

1	1-lb bag washed salad greens
1	handful of each dried fruit: cranberries, cherries, apricots (chopped into 1/2" pieces)
1/4	cup pine nuts or chopped almonds

Your choice of salad dressings, preferably 2 varieties in spritzer bottles

> Empty salad into large, attractive bowl. Add chopped dried fruit to greens. Add chopped nuts. Place spritzer bottles on table next to salad and let guests spritz away.

asian coleslaw

PREP: 15 MIN | SERVES 8-10

With a hint of ginger and other spices, this salad boasts full flavors even though it's made in a flash. From our Asian Delight menu

4	cups finely shredded cabbage (or 2 cabbage and 2 broccoli stalks, shredded)
1	red pepper, cut into julienne strips
2	carrots, grated
4	green onions, chopped
1	cup bean sprouts
1/2	cup chopped coriander, for garnish
1/2	cup chopped peanuts, for garnish

DRESSING

3	tbsp hoisin sauce
3	tbsp rice vinegar
1	tsp granulated sugar
1	tsp soy sauce
1	tsp minced garlic
2	tsp minced gingerroot
2	tsp sesame oil

> Combine first 5 ingredients and place on a large platter. For dressing, combine all ingredients in a clean jar and shake well. Pour over salad on platter and top with reserved garnishes.

grilled caesar

PREP: 15 MIN | COOK: 2-3 MIN
SERVES 6

One of the easiest and tastiest salads we've ever tasted. You might be shocked to learn the romaine is grilled – it's wilted but wonderful! From our Casual Cottage menu

3   romaine hearts
3   slices cooked bacon, cut into bits
1/3   cup shaved Parmesan cheese
1/2   cup croutons

DRESSING
* NOTE: You'll need to make this egg-less Caesar dressing from scratch (no substitutions allowed) because the store-bought variety separates when it hits the hot romaine.
1/2   cup extra-virgin olive oil
1/2   tsp Dijon mustard
1/4   cup grated Parmesan cheese
Juice from 1/2 lemon
1   tbsp red wine vinegar
1/2   tsp liquid honey
1/2   tsp Worcestershire sauce

> Wash and cut romaine hearts in half through the core, careful that the leaves don't separate. Brush cut side of hearts with oil.

> Prepare the dressing by placing all ingredients in a clean jar and shake well. Makes 1 cup

> Place romaine hearts cut-side-down on a very hot 500°F grill and heat for about 1 minute. Don't leave them alone – they only need to char around the edges and wilt slightly.

> Remove hearts from grill and place on serving plates. Drizzle with dressing, top with bacon, Parmesan shavings and croutons.

tip: To make homemade croutons, toss cubes of bread in garlic oil and toast in a skillet on the stovetop until brown. Let cool before adding to salad.

potinis

PREP: 15 MIN | COOK: 20-25 MIN
SERVES 6-8

*A delicious side dish or starter using
'smashed potatoes' and bacon bits.
From our Tuscany at Home menu*

2	lbs baby red potatoes
1	clove garlic, crushed
1/4	cup extra-virgin olive oil

Salt and pepper to taste

1/3	cup grated Parmesan cheese or other hard cheese
1/4	cup chopped fresh parsley, reserve 1 tbsp for garnish
3	oz crumbled cooked bacon

› Scrub the skin of potatoes but do not peel them. Cut potatoes in half, place potato pieces into a pot and add enough water to cover them. Add garlic; we want to add flavor while potatoes are cooking, but remove it before ingredients get combined. Place over high heat and cook until tender and mashable or until the edges of the skins start to curl slightly (you can pierce potatoes with a fork to test readiness). Drain water and remove crushed garlic.

› Using a hand masher or the bottom of a heavy glass, press cooked potatoes flat. Break the skins of the potato but don't over-mash at this point. Drizzle potatoes with oil. Add salt and pepper to taste and toss gently with a fork. Add grated cheese, chopped parsley and most of the bacon pieces, reserving 1 to 2 small pieces for garnish. Mix again with a fork. Spoon potato mixture into bowls or glasses (see tip) and garnish with the reserved bacon and pinches of parsley. Serve warm or at room temperature.

tip: For a stylish presentation, serve in martini glasses or play up the Italian theme by using espresso cups.

asian noodle & shrimp platter

PREP: 15 MIN OR LESS | COOK: 5-7 MIN

SERVES 10-12

Marco Polo couldn't have predicted the freshness of this dish using his precious noodles. The marriage of mint and coriander bring unexpected fragrance and welcomed flavor. From our Asian Delight menu

1	pkg (355 g) thin egg noodles
2	cups coarsely shredded carrots
2	cups seeded peeled cucumbers, cut into julienne strips
4	green onions, chopped
5	cups beans sprouts
1/4	cup chopped fresh mint
1	cup chopped fresh coriander
1	lb frozen large cooked, peeled shrimp, thawed
1/2	cup chopped peanuts (optional)

DRESSING

1/2	cup soy sauce
1	tbsp rice wine
1/4	cup rice vinegar
2	tbsp sesame oil
2	tbsp granulated sugar
1/4	tsp hot pepper sauce

> Cook noodles according to package directions. Drain and rinse with cold water until noodles are cold. Drain well and place in the center of a large serving platter.

> To make the dressing, in small bowl, mix together all ingredients until sugar dissolves. Pour half of the dressing over noodles and toss well.

> Arrange carrots and cucumbers around the outside edge of noodles. Sprinkle green onions on vegetables. Place bean sprouts on top of noodles, sprinkle with mint and coriander. Top with shrimp and peanuts, if using. Drizzle remaining dressing and toss lightly just before serving.

desserts | The perfect way to cool off a heated debate or rev up any discussion. Let them eat cake.

berry bowl

PREP: 10-15 MIN | SERVES 10-12

A healthy, colorful dessert. From our Casual Cottage menu

> Fill an interesting bowl with a variety of fruit, grouping each type and alternating the colors of fruit within the bowl. Serve with Cool Whip or store-bought whipped cream.

tip: Add a dollop of this creamy mixture instead of whipped cream on hot chocolate. Yum!

hazelnut mousse

PREP: 5 MIN | SERVES 8

A tiny sweet treat makes a debut and you take the credit

3/4   cup Nutella spread
1   500-ml container Cool Whip (thawed)
1/4   cup chopped hazelnuts
Chocolate curls for garnish

> Soften the Nutella by beating it with a whisk and fold into the Cool Whip. Serve mousse in 8 Asian soup spoons or shot glasses. Top with hazelnuts and chocolate curls and serve with store-bought amaretti cookies.

designer ice-cream sandwiches

PREP: 15 MIN | SERVES 6-8

Just like designer shoes it's hard to limit yourself to just one...they look so good! From our Tuscany at Home and Casual Cottage menus

1	pint gelato or ice cream
16	thin round biscuit-type cookies (typically 4" in diameter)
1/4	cup chopped nuts or candied fruit

> Soften gelato or ice cream of choice. Scoop ⅓ cup of gelato onto center of cookie, top with another cookie and press together until the gelato moves to edges of cookie.

> Roll the edge of each sandwich into chopped nuts or candied fruit. Freeze for at least 2 hours. See tip for serving suggestion.

tip: You can make these days in advance, but be careful; they may disappear long before your meeting.

gelato parfait

PREP: 5 MIN | SERVES 6

Your guests won't need a passport to savor this Italian favorite that's a perfect finish to any meal.

1	pint chocolate gelato or ice cream
3-6	oz fruit liqueur
Chocolate sauce (optional)	

> Using a melon baller, place 2 to 3 small scoops gelato or ice cream into each of the 6 champagne glasses or other small vessels. Espresso cups work great, too. Return to freezer. Just before serving, remove from freezer and drizzle with ½ to 1 oz liqueur and warmed chocolate sauce, if using.

shortbread

PREP: 20 MIN | COOK: 15 | MAKES 24

A classic from our moms' kitchens.
Served at our "A" Retro Christmas night

1/2	lb salted butter, softened
1/2	cup granulated sugar
2	cups cake and pastry flour

> Combine all ingredients. Rub butter in with fingertips until mixture gathers together and forms a ball; put through cookie press. Decorate with a variety of sprinkles. Bake cookies in a preheated oven at 300°F for 15 minutes or until lightly browned.

sinful chocolate-chip cookies

PREP: 20 MIN | COOK: 8-10 MIN | MAKES 24

A scrumptious soft cookie that's
incredibly chocolatey...any girl's BF

2	cups all-purpose flour
1/2	tsp baking soda
1	tsp baking powder
1/4	tsp salt
2 1/2	(1-ounce) squares unsweetened baking chocolate
1/2	cup butter
1 1/4	cups granulated sugar
2	eggs
1	tsp vanilla extract
2/3	cup sour cream
2	cups semisweet chocolate chips

> Preheat oven to 375°F. Sift together first four ingredients. Set aside. In the microwave or over a double boiler, melt chocolate, stirring until smooth. In a medium bowl, cream together butter and sugar until smooth. Beat in eggs, one at a time, followed by vanilla. Stir in chocolate mixture until well blended. Add sifted ingredients alternatively with sour cream, then fold in chocolate chips. Drop by tablespoonfuls onto ungreased pan. Bake for 8-10 minutes in preheated oven. Let cookies cool before transfering to a wire rack to cool completely. Store in an airtight container.

layer cake with drunken fruit

PREP: 20 MIN | SERVES 8-10

This is an updated version of one of our mother's cheats. Served at our "A" Retro Christmas night

1	cup frozen cherries, thawed
2	oz fruit liqueur
1	rectangular 8"x12" iced frozen cake (preferably chocolate)
2	cups frozen Cool Whip

> In a large bowl, gently mix the frozen cherries with liqueur, careful not to crush the fruit. Set aside.

> Remove the cake while still frozen by running a knife around the edges of the pan and inverting onto a plate covered in plastic wrap. Cut cake in half to form two 8"x6" size cakes. Place one of the cakes, icing side up, onto a great-looking platter that leaves about 2 inches around the perimeter of the cake. Let rest until the icing has thawed.

tip: When putting the two layers together, it works best if the icing is slightly thawed on the bottom cake so they stick together.

> Place the second cake, icing side up, on top of the first one to make a second layer. Spoon half of the container of slightly softened Cool Whip into a small freezer bag and push to one corner of the bag. Cut off the corner and pipe Cool Whip around the bottom edge of the cake where it meets the plate. Pipe around the top edge of the second layer forming a little wall on top of the cake to hold the "drunken fruit" mixture.

> Spoon cherry mixture on top of cake, allowing the liqueur to drizzle down the sides and pool on the plate.

> Option: For a creative effect, you can use the leftover Cool Whip to make little dots or scrolls around the sides of your cake or on top before topping with your drunken fruit.

bavarian apple torte

PREP: 20-30 MIN | COOK: 35 MIN | SERVES 8-10, FREEZES WELL

The secret to this one is not to judge a book by its cover! It may seem like too many steps, but it's easy to make

PASTRY

1/2	cup margarine
1/3	cup granulated sugar
1/4	tsp vanilla
1	cup all-purpose flour

FILLING

1	pkg (8 oz) cream cheese, softened
1/4	cup granulated sugar
1	egg
1/2	tsp vanilla

TOPPING

1/3	cup granulated sugar
1/2	tsp ground cinnamon
4	cups peeled, cored and sliced apples
1/4	cup sliced almonds

> pastry: Cream margarine with sugar and vanilla. Blend in flour. Gather dough together to form a ball. Turn contents into 9" springform pan. Using fingers, press dough evenly over bottom to edges of pan (about ¼ inch thick).

> filling: Combine cream cheese and sugar; mix well. Beat in egg and vanilla until well combined. Pour into pastry-lined pan.

> topping: Combine sugar and cinnamon. Sprinkle sugar-cinnamon mixture over apples and toss until well coated. Spread apples evenly over cream cheese layer. Sprinkle with almonds.

> Bake in a preheated oven at 450°F for 10 minutes. Reduce temperature to 400°F and continue baking for 25 minutes or until apples are cooked. Loosen torte from rim of pan. Let cool before removing rim of pan.

tip: When serving, decorate each piece of pie with a scoop of whipped cream to which you can add a drizzle of liqueur for color.

travel food | Foot-loose and fancy-free, these gems will make your travel menu king of the road.

› shift gears with these tips

- Use brightly colored (and inexpensive) plastic thermal lunch bags to punch up the typical paper-bag lunch.
- Decorate thermal lunch bags with fun stickers. Because we love to recycle, we use the same bags and change the stickers as clues to our secret travel destination.

- Use napkins in different colors and designs. We collect all the extras from our monthly meetings. Pack two or three per lunch bag in case of spills.
- Substitute Chinese take-out containers for the typical paper lunch bag.
- If you plan to munch while in transit, pack crudités, grapes, nuts, cookies and, of course, chocolate!

gg discovery

Because our book clubs have taken us on the road to explore many places, we've learned a few things about preparing meals for our adventurous road trips.

. . . .

❶ Always prepare travel lunches the night before. There's always so many last-minute details to do on the morning of our getaways.

❷ Use 'sippy cups' (plastic cups with lids and straws) when traveling on the road. Pair them with small linen cloths such as a tea towel for a 'lap wrap.' The double strategy helps prevent cranberry and coffee stains.

❸ Individual containers for packed breakfasts/lunches are a must. Passing around a tray of food is risky, especially our signature *GG* Mufflata, which must be individually wrapped.

❹ Remember water! Lots of water, at least one bottle per person each way, along with some flavored crystals (i.e., Crystal Light) for an added change.

traveling triangles

PREP: 15 MIN | SERVES 6-8
MAKES 16 TINY SANDWICHES

These are not your kids' typical lunch sandwiches. Prepared the night before, they make a boxed lunch come alive with flavor

1/2	cup dill-flavored cream cheese
8	slices of thinly sliced pumpernickel bread
8	oz thinly sliced smoked salmon
2	tbsp chopped capers
2	tbsp chopped red onion
1	tsp lemon juice

> Spread a thin layer of cream cheese on each slice of pumpernickel, making sure it covers entire slice. Layer the smoked salmon on top of the cream cheese on 4 bread slices. Mix the capers, red onion and lemon juice together and spread on the smoked salmon. Top with 4 remaining slices. Cut into 4 triangles and wrap in plastic wrap and refrigerate overnight.

tip: Spreading the cream cheese to the edge of each bread slice prevents the bread from getting soggy while chilling overnight. Wrap each sandwich separately using wax paper and curly ribbon to fasten the tiny packages.

chicken 'n' salad

PREP: 25 MIN | SERVES 6

Ideal when there's no time to fuss.
Served on our Niagara getaway

DRESSING

1	cup extra-virgin olive oil
1/3	cup balsamic vinegar
1	clove garlic, minced
1	tsp Dijon mustard
1/4	tsp salt

Cracked pepper to taste

1	3-lb precooked chicken, removed from the bone, or 3 cups cubed cooked meat
4	cups Italian salad mix
1	pint grape tomatoes
1	cup diced cucumber
1	cup halved strawberries
1/2	cup shaved almonds

> Prepare the dressing and set aside.

> Slice the chicken into 2-inch pieces, place in 2-quart Ziploc bag and toss in dressing.

> Combine all remaining salad ingredients and divide into 6 smaller 1-quart Ziploc bags. Before serving, place ½ cup of chicken into each single serving Ziploc bag, seal and toss to mix chicken and greens.

> Empty the bag directly onto a plate. Serve with bread sticks.

tip: Place all the dressing ingredients in a covered jar and shake well. If the ingredients separate, give it a quick shake to emulsify again.

mufflata

 PREP: 25 MIN | SERVES 8-10

No wonder this is a favorite in New Orleans. This make-ahead sandwich is always a crowd pleaser. Served on our Toronto and Vancouver getaways

1	loaf round Italian or long French stick
4	tbsp extra-virgin olive oil
4	tbsp balsamic vinegar
1	6-oz jar prepared (olive) tapenade
8	oz sliced provolone cheese
8	oz each: 4 types of cured meats or cold cuts
1	4-oz jar roasted red peppers
1/4	cup fresh basil leaves

> Cut loaf in half and scoop out center of bread to form two 1-inch think crusts.

> Combine olive oil and vinegar and drizzle over both crusts.

> Spread the tapenade on entire surface of bread crusts. Layer the bottom crust with sliced cheese, meats, then roasted red peppers and basil leaves. Add top crust.

> Wrap the stuffed loaf tightly in plastic wrap and set on a platter or baking sheet in refrigerator with a weight on top of loaf.

> After 8 to 12 hours, remove from fridge, unwrap and slice into 8 to 10 sandwiches. Rewrap sandwiches individually if eating while in transit; otherwise wrap the entire loaf and place in cooler.

tip: Wrap a brick in aluminum foil to use as a weight.

gg bevies

Hosting any event always includes bevies.
Experimentation has led to the creation of the
"booktini." Be spirited, be responsible
and be innovative!

GG favorite booktinis 190 | cool concoctions 194

gg booktinis

GG favorite booktinis | Ways to serve old favorites that promise to delight and refresh guests. All booktini recipes, unless specified, are made in pitchers serving 8 to 10.

> how we do it

We've blended the latest antioxidants with the coolest ingredients; chilled, shaken or stirred, garnished and served, all in the name of creating the newest booktini. The perfect start to any book club meeting.

jeweled
GG james bond

*Ian Fleming would be proud
of this legacy*

15	oz premium gin or vodka
1	oz dry white vermouth
1/4	cup fresh pomegranate seeds

> Add gin, vermouth and pomegranate seeds to a martini shaker filled with ice.

> Shake for 1 minute. The action of the ice bruising the pomegranate seeds will release a fresh burst of flavor. Wait 2 minutes.

> Pour contents into martini glass and add some ice cubes from the shaker.

> **Let me fix you a martini that's pure magic. It may not make life's problems disappear, but it'll certainly reduce their size."** —*Frank Sinatra/Dean Martin, Some Came Running, 1959*

lemon drop booktini

Served with our Tuscany at Home menu

8	oz lemoncello
16	oz vodka
4	oz simple syrup*
8	oz club soda

Thin slice/curl lemon zest

*Simple syrup: combine equal parts water and granulated sugar. Heat and stir until combined. Cool completely before using.

> Mix lemoncello, vodka and simple syrup in a large pitcher filled with ice.

> Stir until container is very cold to the touch.

> Pour into martini glasses garnished with lemon zest.

> Rim preparation: Rub edge of glass with half cut lemon, invert glass into a mixture of grated lemon and sugar.

chocolate-raspberry booktini

What girl doesn't love a little chocolate in her tini

8 oz raspberry-flavored vodka
4 oz white crème de cacao
2 oz Chambord
2 oz Frangelico
Fresh raspberries

> Pour all ingredients except raspberries into a large (*GG* size) martini shaker filled with ice, shake well. Pour into martini glass or glass drizzled with chocolate (instructions follow). Garnish with fresh raspberries.

> Chocolate glass preparation: 1-2 oz each premium white and dark chocolate

> To prepare glasses, don't chill glasses for this booktini. Melt white and dark chocolate in separate shallow bowls in microwave on high for 30 seconds or until chocolate is melted through. Dip rim of martini glass in melted dark chocolate. Use a fork to drizzle white or dark chocolate inside, forming swirls.

tip: Use a wooden skewer to evenly drizzle both types of chocolate in glass.

pear-lychee booktini

Served with our Asian Delight menu

8   oz pear vodka
4   oz pear liqueur
2   oz lychee liqueur
Pitted lychee nuts

> Pour all ingredients except lychee nuts into a martini shaker filled with ice. Garnish with a pitted lychee nut.

stiletto booktini

A favorite at Christmas meetings

8   oz vanilla vodka
4   oz white crème de cacao
2   oz Cointreau
2   oz amaretto
1/2 oz each premium white and dark chocolate (optional)

> Pour all ingredients (except chocolate) into a large (*GG* size) martini shaker filled with ice.

> Shake well. Pour into chocolate-drizzled glasses, if using chocolate. Garnish with cranberries.

 See chocolate-raspberry booktini recipe for chocolate drizzle preparation.

concoctions

cool concoctions | Some standard ingredients make outstanding new creations.

> from simple to splendid

Cool concoctions can spark conversation at book club or any get-together. A little spirit and a dash of creativity helps you light the spark.

pimm's plus

Atonement was never so good

16   oz Pimm's No. 1 Cup
32   oz Orangina or Orange Squash
Ice
Orange slices

> Pour Pimm's gin and Orangina into a pitcher. Stir.

> Pour each serving into an old-fashioned glass half filled with ice.

> Garnish the glass with half slice of fresh orange. Toast the queen and enjoy.

> Serves 8

hottie chocolate

This one works best if made individually for your guests

1/4   cup + 2 tsp granulated sugar, divided
1   tsp ground cinnamon
6   oz premium hot chocolate
     (instant will do)
1   oz butterscotch schnapps
1/2   oz coconut rum
35% whipping cream for garnish
1/4   tsp pure vanilla extract

> Mix together 1/4 cup sugar and cinnamon and place on a flat plate. Rim mug with sugar-cinnamon mixture and set aside.

> Prepare the hot chocolate mixture according to package directions and fill a mug 2/3 full. Add schnapps and coconut rum to hot chocolate.

> In a blender, whip cream until stiff peaks form. Add vanilla extract and remaining 2 tsp sugar. Add a dollop of whipped cream and dust lightly with more cinnamon.

> Serves 1

> *tip:* Add a dollop of the creamy Hazelnut Mousse (**see recipe in Chapter 7, "GG Bites"**) mixture instead of whipped cream on this hot drink. Yum!

hottie toddy

Good for any winter night

30 oz apple cider
16 oz spiced rum
8 oz brandy (optional)
8 oz granulated sugar
Apple slice

> In a large pot, heat cider, rum and brandy over medium heat until bubbles start to form around the edges.

> Rim glass mugs with sugar (see below). Pour warmed liquid into mugs and garnish with apple slice.

> Mug preparation: Dip rim of mug (about 1/8 of an inch) into apple cider, then dip into sugar.

> Serves 8

blueprint | bloo print | noun

1. > a plan or idea that details how something will work
2. > a plan and template for starting a book club, planning a getaway or hosting an event with *GG* panache

blueprints

We've chronicled the makings and growth of our beloved *GG Book Club*, along with our traveling getaway adventures and our fun-loving approach to entertaining. Now it's your turn. Have fun!

book club blueprint

With enthusiasm, commitment and the right mix of women, you can create your own book club. Adopt our blueprint or customize it to your group's needs.

get ready...

get ready

get ready...the members | Open the Pinot Grigio, set out the bites, and get your friends, their friends, neighbors and coworkers together to start the discussion about creating a book club. We'll guide you through some important questions to bear in mind.

Sure, it can be a bit intimidating to start something that takes you outside your comfort zone, but it can be very exciting and rewarding at the same time. There are always excuses for why you think you shouldn't become involved in a book club. Put them aside, be open-minded and, most importantly, relax. This isn't rocket science.

This is an opportunity to get together with other women, enjoy their company, and experience great conversation and great (and sometimes not-so-great) books.

Initially, we had some reservations. Was this going to be more work than fun? What if I hate the books? What if I don't have time for this? But we quickly discovered that all of our concerns were for naught. Now that you agree there are only great reasons to start a book club, let's get going.

 step book club blueprint

Answering these questions will help guide you through the process of building your book club. We've broken them down into three sections.

> get ready...the members

1. Who should join your book club adventure?
2. What is the perfect mix of members?
3. What is the magic number of members?

> get set...the book surprise

4. Do you need a reading list?
5. What type of books should you read?
6. How often should you meet?
7. Where do you find your books?
8. Who leads the book review discussions?
9. Where do you find discussion questions?

> read...the meetings

10. How do you organize your meeting schedule?
11. Where do you meet?
12. What should you serve to eat and drink?

1 | start calling friends, neighbors, friends' friends

Who should you ask to join your book club adventure? Before you can answer this, you need to ask yourself some more questions.

It's important to determine the objectives of your club. What is your reason for meeting? Is it the books? The friendship? The wine? Hopefully, it's all three!

Perhaps now is a good time to tally up the time you spend on yourself. Consider how much richer it would make your life if you had a place – where you can laugh out loud with friends, free from kids, work and partners – and time to call your own. Think about an evening designed purely for your personal enjoyment, without responsibility or worry.

Use our commandments, if only as a guideline, to create your own 'rules.' This is a good starting point for discussing the defining characteristics of your new club. See the *GG* Book Club 10 Commandments in Chapter 1, "Beginnings: Our Book Club Story." There's a lot of room for variation and everyone will naturally have their own preference, but we encourage you to have a common vision for the book club you want to create.

We've stressed it before but it doesn't hurt to repeat: flexibility is very important. However, it needs to be established from the start. So, if one member wants to read only the classics with academic discussion and another is only interested in chick lit, you'll have a problem that even flexibility can't overcome. Whatever your objectives, you'll want members who desire similar – though not exact – styles of reading, discussion and atmosphere to be part of your book club adventure.

2 | find the perfect mix

Create a book club that meets your needs and reflects your interests and that includes members with a similar, but not identical, mindset. Gather an interesting mix of women – friends, old and new; neighbors; acquaintances; coworkers; friends' friends – with an assortment of ages, professions and interests. We find the most important ingredient is members with flexibility and a go-with-the-flow attitude.

3 | discover your magic number

Our magic number is eight to 10 members. We started with six and our group grew to 10. We've found that fewer than six members means that some meetings are too small, making it more difficult for great conversation and animated discussion, especially if someone is absent. As much as everyone moves heaven and earth not to miss a meeting, life does periodically get in the way. So, after much discussion, we decided to increase our size to ensure we had adequate numbers for lively debate. We find any more than 10 members may be unwieldy. If you're a large group, it's difficult to stick to the topic, and to give each member an opportunity to participate in the discussions.

gg discovery

Experience tells us that no fewer than six and no more than 10 members work well. We started as a group of six and have evolved to a group of 10.

· · · · · · · · · ·

get set...the book surprise | Although book club isn't all about books, they do play an important role. We feel the surprise factor is our most important ingredient. Let's walk through the book decisions together.

4 | make it a surprise!

Although we never intended to adopt the element of surprise as a means of selecting our books, it quickly became so. And it has worked out fabulously for us. The member hosting the meeting chooses the book you'll be reading next (not without trepidation, second-guessing and the occasional sleepless night), keeping it a surprise until the end of the evening. This allows our discussions during meetings to be focused on the book at hand without distraction. How a book is presented to members varies – wrapped, not wrapped, in a gift bag, whatever works for the host.

gg discovery

Early on, the GG formula incorporated the element of surprise. It has now become our signature trait that we try to include in everything we do.

. . . .

› consider book list options (or not)

The *GGs* are committed to the element of surprise when it comes to selecting books rather than imposing a book list on its members. Give it a try and see if it works for you. If you're not sold on it, here are other options for creating your reading list.

❶ **Vote on your book list for the year.** Each person brings suggestions to add to the list. The choices are discussed and voted on. The book list is then set for the year.
PROS:
> › Everyone knows what they'll be reading for the year.
> › You can get ahead in your reading when you have extra time.

CONS:
> Everyone knows what they'll be reading for the year.
> If your book isn't chosen, you may be disappointed.
> There's little flexibility to sneak in the latest bestseller.
> There's no opportunity for each person to share her book of choice with the group. This is part of the enjoyment of our book club – introducing something you feel your friends will enjoy.

❷ **Members create a book list.** Each member is able to add one book to the list, depending on the club's framework or guidelines.

PROS:
> It helps give structure to your schedule. A schedule can be created in one of two ways: (1) the book list determines who hosts next, or (2) the hosting schedule determines which book is to be read next. After each person has hosted a meeting, the club creates a new list.

CONS:
> It's missing the element of surprise.
> You'll need to purchase your own book instead of receiving it from your meeting host the way we do.

❸ **Members vote at each meeting on the next book they want to read.**

PROS:
> This approach allows for some element of surprise.
> It allows for spontaneity. Members can go for the latest bestseller.

CONS:
> Everyone is responsible for purchasing her own books.
> Book choice discussions could be long and drawn out.

❹ **Choose books by secret ballot.** At the end of each meeting, members place their votes in a container and select one. Voilà, your choice!

PROS:
> This approach provides an element of surprise.

CONS:
> You'll have to buy your own book.

book genres

action &
adventure

•

biography
& memoir

•

classic literature:
contemporary
& foreign

•

cooking

•

cultural

•

fantasy

•

fiction:
adventure,
contemporary,
crime, historical
& science

•

humor

•

motivational
& inspirational

•

mystery
& suspense

•

personal
growth

•

religion

5 | take it off the bookshelf

Staying true to our concept of surprise and flexibility, the host of our meetings has complete freedom to make her book selection from anywhere on the bookshelf. This allows every member to express her tastes in literature. All genres, authors, themes and subjects are up for grabs. The benefit is that you may read something that you might not have chosen on your own (and love it). We're continually amazed at the number of times this has happened. For a complete listing of our favorite and not-so-favorite reads, see Chapter 2, "On The Bookshelf."

The options are endless when it comes to choosing your book. If you're having trouble getting started consider the sources listed below.

> **Best sellers** – always available and popular

> **Book awards from around the world**
> - **Canada**
>   Governor General's Literary Award aka The GGs
>   Giller Prize
>   Canada Reads
> - **United States**
>   Pulitzer Prize
>   Caldecott Medal
>   Newbery Medal
> - **United Kingdom and Ireland**
>   Man Booker Prize aka Booker Prize
>   Carnegie Medal
> - **International**
>   Nobel Prize for Literature

> **Classics from your university reading lists** – you know, the ones you were supposed to read, but didn't

> The **banned classics** from high school

> Novels from a **favorite author**

> **Books that turned into movies** (then watch the movie together as a group)

> Books with a **specific theme:** life, love, fate, war, mother-daughter or father-son relationships, isolation and exile, women in history, etc.

6 | reading under the covers

The length of your book affects how often you meet. Although this seems like a small issue, it's important, for a number of reasons. One of the key reasons we formed our *GG* Book Club was to get together on a regular basis so we could enjoy each other's company. Based on answers to the questions in this blueprint, we decided that our books should not be greater than 300 pages. This generally allows us to meet once a month with sufficient time to finish each book before the next meeting. It's not a rule, just a guideline. Remember: If the book's page count is too overwhelming and reading becomes a burden, your book club's purpose may be defeated.

7 | go on a book hunt

We use all of the methods listed below to assist us in selecting and buying our books. Our method of choice is as varied as we are. Sometimes a *GG* will choose her book months in advance; other times, she'll make her pick just a few days ahead of her meeting.

> Wander through your favorite bookstore – the big chains, big-box stores or quaint local bookshops. Talk to the staff and look for staff picks.

> Visit websites of different stores and bookstores, including amazon.com, borders.com, chapters.indigo.ca, samsclub.com, walmart.com, target.com and barnesandnoble.com, just to name a few.

> Visit Oprah's website or check out her magazine. She has great picks that typically become instant bestsellers, so they're usually easy to find.

> Read book reviews in newspapers and magazines.

> Listen to book reviews on TV and radio programs.

> Visit your local library for recent book reviews.

8 | questioning questions

At the our meetings, it's usually the *GG* who has chosen the book who also selects the questions and leads the discussion. We're quite relaxed about our discussions and everyone is encouraged to ask questions, if they wish to. It's our goal that everyone has an opportunity to speak. Above all, the ability to listen well, and to allow everyone the freedom to express their point, is critical to the success of any book club.

Here are some other discussion formats to consider:

› Take turns leading prepared questions and discussion

› Have each person prepare one or more questions for each book

› Predetermine the question format for the discussion:
  • Does each member respond to the same question or does each member answer a different question?

› Differentiate between types of questions:
  • literary questions, such as those that deal with language, plot development, narrative voice and author's intent
  • more general questions about enjoying the book and why. For example, what emotional responses did you have to the book?

9 | that's a good question

Good questions help create interesting and thoughtful discussions. However, it can be difficult to come up with one good question that works for every book. So, we mix it up at meetings – delving into more complex literary discussions at times, and adding a dollop of general book questions throughout. You'll need to determine your mix during your initial meeting so everyone's on the same page (no pun intended). There are many resources for book club discussion questions. We've found that our discussions often take on a life of their own. Inevitably, someone will ask a question, followed by the common refrain, "I digress...." We're OK with that and we've not only come to expect it, we embrace it.

❶ For examples of *GG* questions refer to the Top 13 *GG* Book Selections in **Chapter 2, "On the Bookshelf."**

> "A good book is the best of friends, the same day and forever."
>
> —*Martin Tupper*

❷ General sample questions for most books discussions:
- Did you enjoy the book? Why or why not?
- Did the plot pull you into the story or was it a difficult read?
- What was the most important theme of the book?
- Did you like the characters? Could you relate to them?
- What themes were stressed throughout the book?
- What did you learn about yourself and others from the book?
- Did the book end the way you expected?
- If the book was set in another time period, would the outcome be the same?
- If the book was set in another country or culture, would the outcome be the same?
- How did the book compare to others by the same author?
- Did you learn something from the book about another time period, actual event, culture or religion?
- Did the book give a different perspective of an event/person?
- Was the story interesting and compellingly told?
- What were the strengths and weaknesses of the book?

> topics for discussion
> ....
> Background of author
> •
> Book versus movie
> •
> Author's motivation

❸ Literary questions may revolve around structure, characters, themes and settings.
- What was unique about the setting of the book and how did it enhance or detract from the story?
- What specific themes did the author emphasize throughout the book?
- Were the characters fully developed? Did they seem real and believable?
- What do you think the author was trying to convey to the reader?
- How could the book be made better?

❹ Search the Internet for the book author's website. It could have information about the author, as well as book discussion questions and reading guides.

Other resource websites are:
- book-clubs-resource.com
- readinggroupguides.com
- oprahbookclub.com

read...the meetings | This is where all of the fun happens. Our blueprint will take the stress out of preparing for your meeting and help create evenings that will long be remembered.

10 | synchronize calendars, please

Some of our members 'travel' with their work commitments (we hate it when this happens), so we decided to be flexible in scheduling meetings. At each meeting, we synchronize our smartphones or sometimes just fall back on the old-fashioned go-by-memory technique to pick the next meeting date. While we want all members of our group present at each and every meeting because we love their company, it's not always realistic.

We decided that a monthly format, give or take a few days or weeks, works best for us. It offers enough time to read our books and we're more than ready to have another great book club evening by the time the next meeting rolls around. If this relaxed scheduling method does not work for your group, set regular meeting dates and times.

gg discovery

Days after a meeting, the host will send out a quick e-mail reminding the group about the next meeting date to ensure everyone marks it on their calendar.

· · · · · · · · · ·

11 | get out your gps

The comfort of our own homes has been our preferred meeting location. In the beginning, organizing who wanted to host was done simply by asking for volunteers. The order evolved, from asking for the next volunteer to the last woman standing. The original order is now our template for subsequent meetings and has rarely changed.

Other meeting locations
> Bookstore with lounge area or coffee bar
> Café or coffee shop
> Library
> Restaurant
> Outdoor patio

12 | prepare bites and bevies

This is one of our most favorite components of our *GG* Book Club because we love to partake in both eating and drinking. Our meetings have included everything from simple appetizers, to soups and salads, to themed appetizers, to dinners, and everything in between. Our format has become whatever the host wants to serve, taking us back to that 'surprise' element. As with any group, everyone in our little literature-loving crowd is different. Some love to cook and decorate, while others don't. So we have no rules about the format that dictates how bites and bevies are served at our meetings. It really depends on our host, her day and time (or lack of). When it comes time for you to host your book club meeting, check out **Chapter 11, "Hosting Blueprint,"** to assist in your planning.

See Section 3, Bites and Bevies, for fabulous *GG* entertaining ideas, tips and recipes, whether you've got scant time and energy or need the inspiration to make a big splash with a themed evening.

> " Life isn't about how to survive the storm but how to dance in the rain."
>
> —*Dr. Charlotte Robinson*

what to bring to book club

☑ Yourself, ready to relax
and have a great time

•

☑ A great sense of humor

•

☑ Any new wardrobe item
that is dying to get out

•

☑ Trivia and
useful information on
any subject

•

☑ Any item forgotten
at the last meeting

•

☑ A recipe requested
at a past meeting

•

☑ Book being reviewed
for reference

what NOT to bring to book club

☒ Calorie counter
of any kind

•

☒ Handheld devices
(BlackBerries and/or cell
phones with annoying
ring tones should only be
available for scheduling
future meetings)

•

☒ Pictures of the kids,
unless they have just
accomplished something
incredible

•

☒ Cheat sheets

•

☒ Clipboard with yellow
highlighted notes
pertaining to book review

•

☒ Excuses why the book
was not finished (no
excuses necessary)

•

☒ Negative energy
or issues

planning checklist
for book club meeting

. . . .

2 weeks before meeting:

> Make final book selection

> Order online or purchase books

> Determine if this is an opportunity to theme

> If theming, start thinking creatively

1 week before meeting:

> Send an e-mail to remind members about the upcoming meeting. This also acts as a gentle reminder to finish the book

> Consider wrapping your book

gg discovery

Sometimes life gets in the way and you can't finish a book. So remember the *GG* Book Club's 10th commandment: Completing a book is expected, but not mandatory.

. . . .

" Twenty years from now you will be more disappointed by the things that you didn't do than by the ones you did do. So throw off the bowlines. Sail away from the safe harbor. Catch the trade winds in your sails. Explore. Dream. Discover." —*Mark Twain*

getaway blueprint

Our getaways are the cornerstone of our book club and the highlight of our year. Here's our blueprint for exploring new destinations and enjoying new adventures.

get ready...

get ready...the travelers | It's time to get together with your book club sisters, open the Pinot Noir and discuss putting passports on the table.

This new 'chapter' of your book club should start just like its original creation – with open discussion. Talk about traveling together, the adventures you could enjoy and, most importantly, the fun you can have. This is a good time to refer to the *GGs'* **Passport Pledge, see Chapter 4, "Beginnings: Our Travel Story."** Our core purpose, first mentioned in our pledge but worth repeating here, is the reason why our traveling book club exists.

"There is something sacred about a girl's inner circle of friendships. This weekend promises to nurture honesty, strength and trust, and to bestow a lifetime of original and cherished moments on our GG sisters." —GG Passport Pledge

The commitments of our pledge are just for fun, of course. You can use ours or make up your own. Just remember, they set the tone for your getaway, which should be a time to get to know each other better, to bond and create memories together. The purpose of the pledge is actually to get a commitment in spirit to travel from your book club sisters. Agreement to the concept is key to success. Once you've got everyone on board, the excitement will start to build. Now what? Let's explore the basics first.

 20 step getaway blueprint

The questions below will help guide you through the planning of your getaway adventures. They can be broken down into three main sections.

get ready...the travelers

1. Who will plan the getaway adventure?

2. When do you want to travel?

3. How long is the getaway?   4. What is the getaway budget?

get set...the travel surprise

5. Where are you going?

6. How do you get organized?   7. How do you get there?

8. Where do you stay? 9. What do you do?

10. What and where do you eat/drink?

11. How do you create clues? 12. What do you pack?

go...the getaway

13. Planners' Itinerary 14. *GG* Shoe Itinerary

15. *GG* Survival Kit 16. *GG* Travel Kit

17. Travel Tunes 18. Tires-on-the-Road Travel Checklist

19. Up, Up and Away Checklist 20. Planners' Final Checklist

basic getaway checklist

☑ Planners

☑ Date

☑ Number of days away

☑ Travelers

☑ Budget

1 | choose getaway planners

As you've read in previous chapters, we've used different methods to choose our getaway planners, from asking for volunteers to in-house lotteries to old-fashioned parlor games. For details, see Chapter 3, "Best GG Get-togethers." How you decide who plans your next adventure isn't important, as long as you have two planners. Why two? It's no fun to keep a secret to yourself – you need to have a confidante.

After you've picked your planners, the planning can begin in earnest. But before the planners can get down to brass tacks, you'll need some group discussions and decision-making on the basics of the getaway.

2 | synchronize your calendars, please

The first step in planning any book club getaway is to confirm who is able to travel. Being true to the GG goal of flexibility, you need to juggle schedules as much as possible to accommodate everyone's calendars. Even though it can be quite a challenge, you want to include as many of your book club sisters as possible. Once you have a travel date, you need to stick to it.

3 | select the perfect time

The length of time available to travel will determine how far your destination is from home. There is no perfect amount of time. It depends on the individuals in your book club, their work and family commitments, plus their comfort level for travel. For your first trip, a good time frame is a weekend. After that, when everyone has had the time of their lives, members will be motivated to rearrange their schedules for a longer getaway the next time.

gg discovery

Once we agree on a date, we mark it in our calendars in ink. It beces a non-negotiable event because once the planning begins, we need total commitment.

• • • • • • • • •

4 | call the banker

There's a price for everything and coming to terms with that is part of the planning process. Members should agree on a budget early on so everyone is comfortable with the cost of the getaway. There should be no surprises when it comes to money. While the budget can impact the distance you travel, your mode of transportation, accommodation, dining and activities, there's no correlation between budget and fun. More money spent does not necessarily mean more fun. Fun is available at any price.

For our first getaway, we determined the budget by secret ballot. Once we decided to have a weekend getaway, we worked on the cost. We each wrote down the amount we were willing to spend on a weekend away and handed it to our planners. Figuring out an average was simply a matter of adding the figures and dividing by the number of GGs. The planners announced the figure and we agreed. Nothing to think about except the fun in store.

Those members who aren't planning the trip, also known as the travel hostages, can now sit back, relax and look forward to their 'all-inclusive' getaway. They don't have to worry about paying for anything during the trip, except of course personal shopping, which we often squeeze in. Those who commit to traveling give the planners a deposit and don't need to think about money again until the end of the trip. The planners look after all expenses before and during the getaway. It's like being a kid again with someone else seeing to directions, reservations, what to eat and where to go. How much fun is that!?

get set...

get set...the travel surprise | Surprise has not only infiltrated how we select our books but also how we choose our travel destinations. This is all about planning the surprise getaway.

Now the fun begins with the big decision – where to go? Count on your planners to start researching, discussing, considering, reconsidering and analyzing every possible destination. And you thought picking a book was nerve-racking. Of course, the goal is to choose a destination that everyone will enjoy. Picking a destination and the activities for the group is like picking a book – sometimes we are very pleasantly surprised with someone else's selection and we enjoy something we didn't expect to like. How great is that?

The deciding factors for choosing a destination are typically date/availability, length of stay and budget. However, the bigger the budget and length of travel time, the greater the options. Five days on a substantial budget will offer different planning options than two days on a restricted budget.

Start brainstorming ideas of where to go and don't limit your choices – you never know, it may lead to an unexpected destination that you'd never even considered.

sources for where to go
. . . .
> Travel magazines
> City publications
> Travel books
> Websites
> Travel agents
> Newspaper travel sections
> Friends & family

5 | brainstorm getaway destinations

• Big City – North America

Las Vegas, New York City, Chicago, Toronto, Vancouver, Seattle, San Francisco, San Diego, Miami, Montreal, Quebec City, Charleston,

Atlanta, Denver, Los Angeles, Boston, New Orleans, Washington, Savannah, Santa Barbara, just to name a few

- Big City – Europe

London, Dublin, Paris, Amsterdam, Rome, Venice, Madrid, Barcelona, Prague, Vienna

- Wine Country – North America

Napa, Sonoma, Niagara-on-the-Lake, Pelee Island, Washington

- Wine Country – Europe

Tuscany, Piedmont, Loire, Burgundy, Bordeaux

- Cruise

Anywhere in the world

- Fun in the Sun

Mexico, Caribbean, Hawaii, Costa Rica, Florida Keys

- Outdoor Chic

Whistler, Banff, Mount Tremblant, Sedona, Big Sky, Cape Cod

- Spa Resorts

In the desert, mountains, just about anywhere

- Themed Trips

Biking, hiking, horseback riding, kayaking, cooking, cultural, sailing

6 | get organized

Narrow down your destination options to two or three at the most. Too many options can be overwhelming. At this point you need to address your budget again to ensure it can cover all major categories of expense. For example, in some areas, the cost of flights or hotels is high, so there may not be enough left over in your budget for fun activities or dining. If your budget doesn't balance, reconsider some of your options. It's like any budget, household or business: it must balance at the end.

Consider also setting aside a small slush fund for the unexpected, fun activities or diversions along the way in your travels. The unplanned stop for late-night cocktails at the Irish Embassy in our first *GG* getaway is a perfect example. To keep you organized, set up a budget sheet – paper or electronic – with the main budget categories to track and experiment with cost estimates before booking anything.

budget
categories

☑ Transporation

☑ Accommodation

☑ Restaurants

☑ Entertainment

☑ Activities

› create your wish list

Now that you've selected your destination, create a wish list for transportation (car, limo, train, airplane), accommodation (hotel suite, cottage), dining (the choices are endless) and entertainment (theatre, dancing, concerts). Don't forget about adventurous activities (whale-watching or helicopter riding). Use the web, city reference publications and magazines to help you make selections.

    With so many details to plan and track, we've created planning tools, complete with instructions, to facilitate the process. It's like a puzzle, with each planning component requiring its own set of decisions. Visit our website readingbetweenthewines.ca and check out our handy templates.

7 | travel in planes, trains, limos, boats and vans

How are you going to get there? It depends on where you're going and your budget. Consider all methods for booking transportation (both travel agent and online) to ensure you don't blow your budget. Arriving in a limo can be exciting, but if it means there are no funds left for fun activities, you've defeated the purpose of your getaway. On our first getaway to Toronto, we had no extra dollars for trains, planes or limos – just our trusty minivan. That worked out fine because that left more money for fun and frivolity.

a penny saved

consider renting:
> a cottage in the country
> an apartment or condo in the city
> a one- or two-room suite in a hotel
> a time-share property

8 | enjoy home base

Where are you going to crash at the end of every fun-filled day? Your home base, or home away from home, is one of the most important considerations of your getaway. Cost and location are key factors. Although a central location may cost a bit more, it may be well worth it for the convenience of being closer to the action. This will save time and money for cabs. Think of your wish list of activities and choose your accommodation accordingly.

home base activities
Talking, laughing, relaxing, kicking back, napping/sleeping, drinking booktinis and wine, eating bites, drinking coffee, grabbing a quick brekkie

9 | remember...girls just want to have fun

The options for activities are endless, based on your group's interests. We've tried to choose activities that we wouldn't typically do on a regular family vacation. Because fun means different things to different people, we try to have an assortment of choices. For example, we all enjoy shopping but had never been on a shopping tour. We all eat out, but none of us had ever dined at an Ethiopian restaurant. Here are some ideas to consider as you select your getaway activities.

> getaway activity ideas

- > Market and food tours
- > Cooking classes and demonstrations
- > Dining – over-the-top, casual and ethnic
- > Shopping extravaganzas – quaint streets, organized tours, malls or factory outlets
- > Retreats
- > Outdoor activities – biking, kayaking, horseback riding, sailing, golfing, mountain biking and skiing (downhill or cross-country)
- > Get cultured – art galleries/shows and museums
- > Walking tours – city and country
- > Sightseeing – walking, bus, helicopter, limo and train
- > Spa treatments
- > Theatre
- > Book events such as author readings
- > R&R by the pool
- > TV show set visits
- > High and casual tea

10 | go out or stay in

What and where do we eat and drink? This is always an important question for the GGs because we all enjoy both. We mix it up, trying out restaurants that are not available in our city. It's always great to have an interesting combination – some ethnic, some casual and some more formal dining options.

> reservations, please

You're on an adventure, so be adventurous. We always try to have one over-the-top dining experience – something special – on our trip, usually saved for the last evening. Go online, read reviews and make reservations. It's easy. If you can't make up your mind, make reservations at a couple of places and cancel one when you've made a final decision.

> room service, please

We also enjoy relaxing and having bites and bevies at our home base. Sometimes it's just a quick Booktini before we head out for the evening. Other times we crash for the night, just too tired to go out. (It's hard to believe, we know, but it happened in Vancouver.) So then we relax, enjoy our late-night bites and regain our strength for the next activity-packed day. We also plan for coffee and breakfast at home base. This saves both time and money.

11 | create a clue box

We use a clue box to give our hostage GGs hints about the planned destination and activities. Each set of planners can customize the clue box as they wish. We've certainly used it in a few different ways.

gg discovery

It's wise to have a few dining options in your home-base neighborhood. After a long and exciting day, getting into a cab to go across the city isn't always that much fun.

. . . .

We've created individual boxes or bags for each traveler, distributed at our departure point or waiting on the seats for them in our getaway vehicle. Some planners have had pre-getaway meetings in which they assess the clues over cocktails. Each traveler approaches her clue box differently, just like children do when opening a birthday present. Some tear into the box, pulling everything out at once, while others remove the clues one by one and carefully assess them. There's rapid-fire discussion and analysis. Who will guess first? It's not often that someone guesses correctly and if they do, the planners still won't tell.

For our Vancouver getaway, we created one large box to hold all of the clues and passed it around for each traveler to assess. We used the box as a teaser at our book club meeting a few weeks before our trip and then again upon our departure. It was a clue refresher that encouraged guesses, and a test to see if anyone was any closer to the final answer.

Clue boxes are simple to make. Use a shoebox, purse, party bag, anything that holds a multitude of trinkets and fun finds. Look for clue objects around your house or at the local dollar store. Think about your getaway's landscape and landmarks, dining locales, planned activities or teasers to throw the hostages off-course when guessing. Use your imagination and have fun.

12 | laundry quandary

How do you tell the travel hostages what to pack without giving away the destination and activities? The *GGs* have devised the perfect method – a shoe packing list. This little bit of innovation simply lists the types of shoes to bring – no more, no less. Now it's up to the hostages to match up the appropriate clothing with the shoe list.

> **what to wear?**
> Our hands-down, best travel outfit for comfort and versatility is: yoga pants/capris, jacket and T-shirt (our favorite is Rethink Target shirts).

There are often airline restrictions on luggage weight and limited space in vehicles. Because of this, we try to keep our luggage to a minimum and our sharing to a maximum. So...

- one or two of us brings a blow dryer;
- we leave the big bottles of hair-care products at home or bring travel sizes. Most hotels have shampoo and conditioner in each room;
- we're prepared to share shoes, clothes, jewelry and accessories;
- and the planners bring the *GG* Travel Kit and *GG* Survival Kit for essential items anyone might need.

> **When preparing to travel, lay out all your clothes and all your money. Then take half the clothes and twice the money."** —*Susan Heller*

P.S. When you're on a traveling book club getaway, you don't have to take twice the money. Travel hostages don't take any money. Remember, all you do is show up and have fun!

go...the getaway | Now it's time to go.
Use our suggestions to ensure a fabulous,
flawless getaway.

We can't emphasize enough the need for organization.
It minimizes the getaway stress for the planners so they
can enjoy the trip, too. Our key to success has been the
use of checklists. Here, we've included several, to be used as is or
adjusted to your needs.

13 | complete the planners' itinerary

Now it's almost time to go. Just a few more
things to do to ensure a stress-free execution
of your trip. By this time, you've invested
many hours in the planning of your getaway
and have your hostages anxiously awaiting
the outcome.

Because you've diligently followed steps
1 to 12 of your getaway blueprint, you have
all the key details listed on your planners'
itinerary: date, time, accommodation,
activities and dining, including phone numbers
and e-mail addresses for easy communication.

› get organized

Make a couple of copies of the planners' itinerary for each planner. It
would be a disaster to lose your only copy – it would be like losing your
day planner at work. But be careful not to let any of the hostages see the
itinerary – that would be like the kids finding your Christmas gift-shopping
list. Also, make copies of e-mails, confirmation and reservation details,
plus maps, especially if you want to follow up a confirmation. We usually
keep all of our papers in a plastic file folder.

⟩ account for costs

Because the planners are responsible for making this an "all-inclusive" trip, some bookkeeping is necessary. The planners can share the responsibility or assign it to the most fiscally responsible. Some love bookkeeping, others don't! We try to prepay as much before departure by credit card. This just eliminates one more thing to be thinking about during the trip. As a planner, you want to have a great time too, and not constantly be checking bills for different activities.

Bring Ziploc bags for your daily receipts. Before you place them in the bag, write the activity right on the receipt so you're not guessing what it was for when you get home. This keeps everything organized in a simple format.

14 | GG shoe itinerary

After all of this secretive planning, how do the hostages know when and where to be, wearing the appropriate clothing? As you know by now, no one ever knows what they'll be doing until they're actually doing it. The planners heading up each trip handle the big reveal a bit differently. Sometimes we provide a *GG* Shoe Itinerary, handed to the travelers just as we arrive at our destination. It lists the times everyone needs to be standing at the front door, ready for action, wearing the appropriate shoes. In lieu of a shoe itinerary, some planners hand out beautiful cards each morning that hold clues to the day's activities, in addition to the essential shoe requirements and time of departure.

---

gg shoe itinerary

Toronto, Ontario

Please be at the hotel door, promptly, at the time listed, wearing appropriate footwear.

Friday...

5:00 p.m.	2" heels (good to look at but you may regret it)
7:00 p.m.	no time to change

...Sunday

9:00 a.m.	Flats or 1" heel or anything that still feels good
10:30 a.m.	It might be time to trade shoes with your roommate
12:00 p.m.	Same as 9:00 a.m.
2:00 p.m.	No matter what you're wearing, if your tired little guys are crying, loosen up!
4:00 p.m.	Let those guys see the light of day if you think they need a break!!!

15 | GG survival kit (medical travel kit)

You can waste a lot of time in a strange city looking for the basics. So, we recommend you bring the 10 must-have medical essentials with you. One kit will do for all the travelers. If anyone has special medical requirements, remind them to bring along their own medication and/or prescription.

1. Advil, Tylenol or any extra-strength pain medication – for sore heads and feet and everything in between
2. Gravol – for train, boat and automobile adventures
3. Tums or any antacid remedy – exotic food sometimes requires it
4. Imodium – just to be prepared
5. Cold medication – it never fails, when you finally get away on a holiday, that's when a cold strikes
6. Sore throat lozenges
7. Antihistamine medication
8. Multivitamins – to keep you strong, ready for fun
9. Melatonin – to adjust to jet lag
10. Nytol – for those long flights

17 | travel tunes

There's nothing like a great playlist to get everyone revved up during your getaway road trip. And more than just provide entertainment, your playlist can multitask. The songs you pick can provide clues for your destination or distractions along the way, all the while motivating the songstresses in your group to strike a chord as you head down the highway. These tunes also make for great pre-bedtime dancing (if you have an ounce of energy left). Make your own CDs or iPod playlists of your favorites.

16 | GG travel kit

Here's our 10 must-have, can't-travel-without items.
In the interest of saving weight and space in your luggage, the planners assemble the travel kit for everyone to share on the trip. You're now prepared for most eventualities. What is the point of everyone having to carry duplicates of everything?

1. Corkscrew
2. Hand sanitizer
3. Disposable wet cloths – for those sticky situations
4. Band-Aids and liquid Band-Aid – for those poor, tired feet
5. Tide pen or Oxyclean wipes – for those coffee spills
6. Sewing kit – including safety pins
7. Nail polish remover
8. Sunscreen – assorted strengths
9. Eye covers – for your beauty rest
10. Earplugs – consider this a preventive measure. Remember Passport Pledge # 1 – I will share a bed and cold feet and will tolerate snoring without complaint

> favorite 12 GG travel tunes

1. Big & Rich • Comin' to Your City 2. Tom Cochrane • Life is a Highway
3. AC/DC • Highway to Hell 4. Steppenwolf • Magic Carpet Ride
5. Bryan Adams • Run to You 6. Queen • We Will Rock You
7. Big & Rich • Save a Horse, Ride a Cowboy
8. Sheryl Crow • All I Wanna Do Is Have Some Fun
9. Cyndi Lauper • Girls Just Want to Have Fun
10. Nelly Furtado • Maneater 11. Ok Go • Here It Goes Again
12. AC/DC • It's a Long Way to the Top

18 | tires-on-the-road travel checklist

If you're traveling by car, SUV or van, get ready for a carefree road trip getaway. Don't leave home without reviewing these two checklists.

no-brainer car essentials

- Driver's license
- Vehicle registration and insurance
- Full gas tank
- Clean car – inside and out. Not necessary, but here's a good excuse to actually get it done
- Tune up or at the very least have the basics checked: tires, oil and other fluid levels
- Extra oil and windshield wiper fluid in the trunk
- Roadside assistance info from car dealership or CAA/AAA

GG 10 essential essentials

1. Cellphone – planners only
2. Map, MapQuest directions and/or GPS
3. Cheaters – if needed to read the map
4. Cooler filled with travel bites and bevies – see **Chapter 7, "GG Bites" and Chapter 8, "GG Bevies"** for ideas
5. Napkins and wet wipes
6. Water – unfortunately, this can lead to several pit stops
7. Bevies – for instant cocktail hour upon arrival
8. Road trip travel tunes CD – gets everyone in the mood for travel
9. Coffee – everyone needs coffee for a road trip
10. Après-coffee mints

gg discovery

Be prepared with a coffee lap-wrap – keep a few tea towels in your car. Place them on your lap while drinking coffee, tea or juice and save your clothing from spills.

. . . .

19 | up, up and away checklist

Before jetting off to the airport, don't forget
to check for:

- ☑ Valid passports
- ☑ Airline e-tickets and preprinted boarding passes
- ☑ The bevie allowance
- ☑ Travel lunch and/or snacks

20 | planners' final checklist

To be checked and rechecked before departure

- ☑ Planners' itinerary for planners' eyes only. Bring two copies each.
- ☑ Money and bookkeeping folders/bags
- ☑ *GG* Shoe Itinerary
- ☑ *GG* Travel Kit, packed
- ☑ *GG* Survival Kit (Medical Travel Kit) packed
- ☑ Clue box or boxes
- ☑ Lunch, prepared and packed
- ☑ Travel tunes

airline issues

Because regulations are always changing, check with your airline for luggage restrictions, including those for carry-on bags. Check for the size, weight and number each passenger is permitted.

hosting blueprint

· ·

Dip into unchartered waters with
our tricks, tips and cheats to help you get
ready with time to spare.

get ready...

get ready...you're hosting | It's your turn to host. Our blueprint will help you get organized, be creative and make hosting a breeze.

Follow our 12 easy steps to help plan your evening. Get started using our proven tips and invaluable checklists. You'll be amazed how quick and easily it all comes together.

1 | now it's your turn

It's your turn to host and that means, among the many looming decisions required of you, it's time to choose a book for review. Just refer to Chapter 9, "Book Club Blueprint" for ideas on how, what and where, so you can make the perfect choice.

One task down, one to go. The next to-do involves planning your evening – to theme or not to theme? It's up to you. Some books offer perfect opportunities to theme, while other books are just about impossible. Maybe there simply isn't the time to coordinate a theme. So be it. Do whatever works best for you when hosting.

2 | pantry+planning=bites

It's time to create your menu. In *GG* terms, that means finalizing your bites selections. See Chapter 7, "*GG* Bites," along with cookbooks and magazines for ideas and inspiration. Have fun creating your menu. Theming might help you narrow down your menu choices. Many of us

12 step hosting blueprint

Having thoroughly enjoyed book club meetings hosted by others, now it's your turn to entertain your book club sisters. Break down tasks, do some prep work and you'll be ready to go.

› get ready...you're hosting

1. What is your book choice?
2. How do you create a bites menu?
3. How do you create a bevie menu?
4. What are your serving requirements?

› get set...the week before

5. What do you need to buy?
6. When do you prepare the bites?
7. What needs a quick polish?
8. What playlist do you use?
9. How do you arrange your meeting space?

› go...the meeting day

10. What last-minute bites and bevies do you need?
11. When do you open the wine? 12. What's left to do?

gg discovery

There's nothing like the supportive environment of a book club meeting to experiment with new ideas. Never cooked Asian? Give it a shot.

· · · · · · · · · ·

enjoy entertaining while others simply don't have the time or inclination. Don't discount the option of take-out or frozen hors d'oeuvres – either is acceptable. We've said it before, but we'll say it again: it's not about the food. Do whatever works for you.

Wherever you measure on the hosting meter, everyone needs some shortcuts along the way. We've created *GG* 101 lists to assist you in your everyday menu planning and to make hosting your book club meeting as easy and stress-free as possible.

What's best, these lists work for everyone, whether you have little or no interest in cooking, love to cook or fall somewhere in between. The lists are meant to be used as guidelines. We aren't saying you need to have all of these items on hand; these lists are just a reference to help you create your menu. It's like a mix-and-match outfit – pick a few components, then pair them up as they appeal to you.

Head to your kitchen and take stock of your supplies. Then make a shopping list using the *GG* 101 lists and the recipes you've selected.

GG Pantry 101
From grocery shelf to pantry shelf to table

Staples: all three ingredients make anything taste better

- Olive oil – a good quality extra-virgin olive oil is best
- Vinegars – balsamic, red, wine, rice wine
- Sea salt – plain or flavored

Condiments: use to add flavor

- Red pepper jelly
- Antipasto mix, bruschetta mix
- Fig spread
- Chutney
- Salsa – original or fruit
- BBQ or teriyaki sauce
- Seafood sauce

Nuts: go well on cheese platters or alone for nibbling

- Candy coated
- Pistachios, macadamia, cashews, almonds, pine nuts
- Mixed

Breads & Crackers: perfect with any cheese, dip or condiment

- Baguettes – white or whole wheat
- Lesley Stowe's Raincoast Crisps
- Cheese sticks, dried bread sticks, crostinis
- Rosemary and sea-salt crisps
- Flatbread crisps
- Pumpernickel

Chips: nothing more to say, everyone's guilty pleasure

- Potato chips – any of the great new flavors
- Corn tortilla chips – blue or white
- Chili lime tortilla chips
- Vegetable chips

Dessert: just open and plate

- Truffles or chocolates
- One-bite brownies or cookies

GG Fridge 101
From grocery cooler to fridge to table

Dips: perfect with vegetables and crackers
- Grilled red pepper
- Asiago artichoke
- Garlic hummus
- Tzatziki
- Baba ghanouj

Pâtés: a nice addition to a cheese tray
- Salmon
- Rustic peppercorn

Cheeses: serve on a cheese tray with fruit and baguettes or portion and serve with a condiment on a cracker
- Yorkshire Wensleydale cheese with cranberries
- Blue cheese with pear
- Brie
- Cambozola
- Goat cheese log
- Parmesan
- Cream cheese
- Caramelized onion cheddar

Olives: perfect with cheese, meats, pâté or alone
- Spicy
- Stuffed
- Assorted

Meats: go well with cheese, olives, baguettes
- Prosciutto
- Salami
- Serrano ham
- Capicola

Fruit & vegetables: go well with everything except chips
- Arrange in pre-made portions or on trays

Soups: pair with a salad and you have an instant meal
- Wild mushroom soup
- Brie butternut squash soup

GG Freezer 101
From grocery freezer to home freezer to table

Ready-to-serve appetizers or just bake and serve
- Smoked salmon
- Shrimp ring
- Coconut shrimp
- Meatballs, sausage rolls, rumaki
- Asian appetizer assortment – spring rolls, dumplings
- Assorted appetizer combos – phyllo, puff pastry

Desserts: instant wow, just add strawberries and truffles
- Mini cream puffs or mini chocolate éclairs
- Cheesecake

Here are some sample menus we've created with items from the GG 101 Lists

Mediterranean 🍽 Menu
prosciutto, parmesan cheese and grape platter
assorted olives
dips: antipasto, asiago-artichoke
sliced baguette and assorted crackers
goat cheese and fig phyllo appetizer

Retro 🍽 Menu
shrimp ring with seafood sauce
veggies and dip
assortment of chips and nuts
hot appetizers: meatballs in BBQ sauce,
sausage rolls and rumaki
mini cheesecake bites

Instant 🍽 Bites
The easiest way to serve great bites at book club is to call your favorite restaurant, order your favorite items and pick them up on your way home from work. Voilà. It's up to you whether you want to tell your fellow members your secret.

important GG booktini rules

. . . .

A perfect booktini should be a fabulous jewel tone. If a drink isn't see-through, it's NOT a booktini, but a cocktail.

•

1. Only serve one; two if it's a special occasion. Beware if offering more!

•

2. Use only key ingredients listed in the *GG Booktini Tool Kit*.

•

3. Chill everything: glasses, shaker and spirits, either by adding ice to glass before using or placing glasses in freezer.

•

4. Prepare booktinis by the batch in advance and chill in the freezer in a martini shaker. Serve when your book club sisters arrive – just re-shake and pour over ice.

3 | no bartender required

Our *GG Bevie Pantry 101* will assist you with your bevie selection and planning as you prepare to host your book club. Bevie choices are often easy to match with your book choice. The book you've selected might mention a specific drink or wine, or you might want to match your bevie with the country or area where the story is set or the particular era in which it takes place.

For example, a mint julep is mentioned in *Divine Secrets of the Ya-Ya Sisterhood*, Italian wine and lemoncello pair well with *Under the Tuscan Sun*, Perrier water and champagne from France work well with *Almost French*, Chinese tea is a natural fit for *Mao's Last Dancer* and martinis are a great match for the book *Without Reservations*. The possibilities are endless with a little imagination!

Our bevie pantry list covers the basics, along with a few extras to help you make a splash when serving bevies. We include booktini and wine essentials in our *GG Bevie Pantry 101*, and because it's important to have nonalcoholic options available, various waters, coffee and tea choices also make the list.

We've even included a tool kit to arm you with the essentials for making a perfect *GG* booktini, whether you choose one of ours from **Chapter 8, "GG Bevies"** or create your own.

In addition to the influence your book choice might have on theming, your choice of wine may inspire your menu. For those practicing sommeliers, refer to our "Easy Steps to Select Wine" and "Quick Guide to Food and Wine Pairings" sections later in this chapter. Now all that's left to do is to get busy stocking up.

P.S. Don't forget the ice

If you have an ice maker in your freezer and don't use it often, store older ice in a plastic bag and use it to chill white wines and martini glasses. You won't want to use it in drinks – ice that sits too long in your freezer can take on the flavors of the foods stored along with it. Prepare ice for drinks ahead of time. There's nothing worse than a warm martini. If you've left it too late, pick up a bag at the convenience store.

GG Bevie Pantry 101

Booktini/cocktail essentials:
- Martini glasses
- Martini olives stuffed/flavored with:
    - › jalapeño › sun-dried tomato › vermouth › blue cheese
    - › juniper berries › Spanish garlic with curry
- Olive picks
- Fun cocktail napkins
- Drink rimmers such as coarse salt and lemon-infused sugar
- Cocktail mixers
- Key ingredients (see *GG Booktini Tool Kit*)

Wine essentials:
- Wine glasses
- Ice bucket
- Red Wine
- Wine jewelry, markers
- Corkscrew
- White Wine

Wonderful waters:
Flavored water
- Sweet lime cordial
- French lemonade
- Ginger & lemongrass cordial
- Rose's Lime cordial

Sparkling water and natural water
- San Pellegrino
- Evian
- Bling H2O
- Perrier
- Fiji

Coffee:
- Flavored
- Organic

Tea:
- Herbal, Red, White, Green, Black

Ice: from your fridge door, freezer or convenience store

❝ **There comes a time in every woman's life when the only thing that helps is a glass of champagne.**❞ —*Bette Davis* (**In Old Acquaintance**)

> GG Booktini Tool Kit

Martini glasses	An eclectic collection replaces the need for glass charms
Martini shaker	Required equipment to prepare the perfect 'tini
Olive picks	Used to skewer the giant gourmet olives or whatever captures your imagination
Shot glass or measuring cup	Essential when making 'tinis by the batch
Ice	You can never have enough
Key ingredient #1 • spirits	Endless choices of fab-flavor-infused spirits
Key ingredient #2 • any clear liqueur(s)	The magic ingredient that can make a difference in taste and color. The unique combo of ingredients and proportions determines the intensity of flavor
Garnish	Place this finishing ingredient on picks or float in the glass

tip: The key to a fabulous booktini is to serve it COLD, ice cold. Keep the ingredients and martini shaker in the freezer until needed. The glasses can go into the freezer too. If that doesn't work logistically, fill your glasses with ice before you start making the 'tinis.

› Martini Lingo

James Bond Classic	A traditional 2 oz gin with a very small splash of dry vermouth
On the rocks	Over ice in the glass
Straight up	No ice in the glass
Shaken, not stirred	The 'tini is shaken vigorously in the shaker, not gently stirred. The force of the ice crashing in the vessel determines the amount of air released from the ice, a process that's rumored to be the secret behind a great martini.

> 66 I am prepared to believe that a dry martini slightly impairs the palate, but think what it does for the soul."
> —*Alec Waugh*

› easy steps to select wine

In the more than 60 *GG* Book Club meetings, we've learned a few things about selecting the perfect wine for the night. We apply the book club and getaway mantra to making our wine picks: relax and have fun. Feel free to experiment.

here are our tips:

› food and wine pairings

Consider what food you'll be serving when making your wine choice. Your wine should complement your menu, not compete with it. A wine shouldn't be so full bodied that it might overpower a shrimp mousse, and not so sweet that is doesn't complement crudités and dip. Will it stand up to the variety of flavors and dishes? It's best to aim for balance. A Cabernet might be too full bodied for mild cheeses. A Sauvignon Blanc might not be bold enough to pair with an aged cheese or garlic-flavored dip. Refer to our "Quick Guide to Food and Wine Pairings" section.

› red or white

Select a house wine that has diversity, instead of picking wine for each food item or course. There are lots of choices, so it's best to narrow your pick to one red and one white. The ratio of red and white is up to the hostess, and her familiarity with what her guests prefer.

› price

Wine comes at many price points and you can spend as little or as much as you want. However, a higher price doesn't guarantee a better wine. Determine how much you want to spend and look at the options at that price. There are lots of great finds between $10 and $15.

> ## research

There are endless resources about wine and it can be overwhelming. Like everything else that we talk about, keep it simple. The experts at your local wine store are a fabulous resource. Tell them your menu and price point and ask for suggestions. Ask a friend what they recommend or research the Internet. When all else fails make your choice based on the cool label.

> ## quantity

A 750-ml bottle will serve five glasses of wine. How many bottles should you purchase? You are the best judge as you know your guests – some will only have one glass while others will enjoy more. It's always better to have a little extra to avoid running out halfway through the evening. You can always return unopened bottles or keep them for another occasion.

> ## temperature

One common mistake with wine revolves around serving temperature. White is usually served too cold, directly from the fridge and red is typically served too warm, at room temperature. According to the pros, white wine should be chilled, and then served 20 minutes after removing it from the refrigerator. Red wine should be slightly cooler than room temperature, chilled for 20 minutes in the refrigerator before serving.

> ## glassware

Keep it simple. Choose a wine glass that works with either red or white. Don't worry about the type of glasses you use. Just make sure they're squeaky clean, freshly polished and free of lint.

gg discovery

Take the white wine out of the fridge, put the red in, wait 20 minutes, enjoy both. Use this rule of thumb and you'll always be close to the perfect temperature for most of your wine choices.

· · · · · · · · · ·

> quick guide to food and wine pairings

There are many considerations to bear in mind when selecting a wine, including acidity, region, body and grape type. However, the current philosophy of many wine experts is that there is no right or wrong answer to matching food and wine. As with books and getaways, the possibilities are endless. So throw away the rule book, improvise and enjoy.

One simple rule: lighter food, lighter wine; heavier food, heavier wine.

Here's an at-a-glance guide to basic food-and-wine pairings to help you in your selections.Before you know it, you'll be an expert matchmaker of food and wine.

White Wines
• Chardonnay is wide-bodied with a velvety citrus flavor, as well as buttery notes. It goes well with seafood, chicken, rich soup, goat cheese and other strongly flavored cheeses and cream sauces.
• Sauvignon Blanc is a versatile wine great for drinking on its own or serving with food. It goes well with poultry, seafood and salad.
• Gewürztraminer has a fruity flavor with peach, rose and allspice overtones. It's great with Asian food.
• Riesling is a fresh, light wine with fresh apple flavors. It pairs well with chicken, fish and pork, mild cheeses, and Indian and Asian foods.

Red Wines
• Merlot is considered an easy-to-drink wine that serves as a good introduction to red wine. Merlot can be served with any type of food.
• Cabernet Sauvignon has a full-bodied flavor, drawn from perhaps one of the world's best varieties of grape. Cabernet Sauvignon is often served with red meat, cheddar and blue cheese.
• Pinot Noir works well with salmon and tuna, and leaner meats such as veal and chicken. Consider chilling slightly to maximize the peppery, earth-tone qualities.
• Zinfandel is a versatile grape, used to make wines from blush to full-bodied reds. It has a zesty berry and pepper flavor that goes well with roast beef, poultry and pasta.
• Shiraz is fruity with tastes of black pepper. It pairs nicely with beef, stews and wild game.

Sparkling Wines
• Champagne and sparkling wines are great accompaniments to fancy hors d'oeuvres, sushi and omelettes.

4 | presentation is everything

Your next step is to take inventory of all the dishware that you'll need for the evening. This includes tableware, cutlery, serving pieces and glassware. This may sound very tedious but it's important for a number of reasons. It helps you to determine the quantity of items required and to assemble the best presentation for your bites and bevies. It also saves you from running to the kitchen during your meeting to grab an extra item, only to discover that you don't have it. There's nothing worse than trying to find the perfect serving dish when the doorbell is ringing. You'll be amazed at how store-bought dips and appetizers transform from boring to beautiful in seconds simply by placing them in your own dishes or on your own trays. Be imaginative. Use an unexpected container or unique serving piece that works with your theme. This is a simple way to add fun to your food.

gg discovery

If you're short on anything, consider borrowing from a friend. On the other hand, if it's something you think you might use more often, consider purchasing it.

· · · · · · · · · ·

get set...

get set...the week before | It's getting closer, but don't worry: you'll be in total control with these tips.

Your turn to shine as host is only one week away. While everything should be under control, there are a few more items you'll need to check off your lists.

5 | hit the grocery aisle

With list in hand, prepare to take a very organized trip to the store. Some like to do it all in one trip; others break it up into different trips and different stores. Do whatever works for you. Don't forget your list and your re-usable shopping bags.

6 | chop, slice, dice

Prepare as much food as possible in advance to reduce last-minute stress and panic. If any of your recipes can be prepared a day ahead of time, take advantage of this! See recipes in **Section 3, Bites & Bevies,** and the suggestions in our *GG* **101** lists in this chapter to get you ready.

7 | borrow, wash and polish

If you need to borrow, don't leave it until the day of your meeting. Wash and polish all dishes, silverware and glassware. Have them set aside, ready to go to set the table or appetizer area.

8 | plug in the iPod

Music is important in creating the evening's ambiance and adding to a theme. The room can instantly take on the character of the music, springing to life as a Parisian bistro, an Italian opera or an exotic Chinese scene. Or let the music set the time period – big band swing versus the Beach Boys versus Michael Bublé. Haven't got a theme? No worries, play your current favorite playlist softly in the background.

Load up your iPod with your preferred tunes, find a foreign radio station on satellite or gather your CDs and let your audio system do the rest.

9 | prepare & conquer

> Set the table for dining or appetizers

It's amazing how much more relaxed you feel when you've organized your meeting area. Set the table ahead of time so you can make last-minute changes or add some decorative touches if you wish. Anything can happen the day of book club – problems at work, changes in kids' schedules or car troubles, so cover your bases.

Make sure you've got enough seating for everyone, with either chairs or comfy pillows so every member is comfortable and ready for some lively conversation and debate (always friendly, of course).

> Is your front hall closet ready to receive guests?

Where are you going to put the coats? Sometimes, it's dangerous just opening the front hall closet. If that's the case in your home, have an alternate location, or grab extra hangers from other closets to make room for extra coats and jackets. Book club shouldn't mean more work just a little creative shuffling!" Remember this is a fun night.

> Don't forget your books

If you're planning to wrap your book for the big reveal, give yourself plenty of time to pick up the right gift wrap, ribbon, stickers, whatever. Refer to **Chapter 1, "Beginnings: Our Book Club Story,"** for book-wrapping suggestions. If you're not wrapping your books, make sure that they are tucked away and out of sight until you distribute them (just don't forget where you put them, so they don't suffer the same fate as those Christmas presents that turn up during spring cleaning).

go...the meeting day | There are just a few last-minute things to do. Answer the door, relax and have fun.

10 | remember last-minute stuff

Finish all of your last-minute bites and bevies preparation. Complete the plating of all your appetizers so you're able to greet guests without stressing about no food being on the table. Have the welcome booktini chilling in the fridge.

11 | uncork the wine

Open the wine before guests arrive so you aren't fighting with corks at the last minute. Open both the red and white before guests arrive. The red can breathe and the white can warm up a bit.

12 | set the mood

What's left to do?

- turn on the music and adjust the volume
- dim the lights – there's nothing worse than being under a spotlight
- light the candles
- ensure that books are in their rightful place and ready to go

Answer the door...relax and have fun!

66 **One's destination is never a place, but a new way of seeing things."** —*Henry Miller*

› GG book club hosting checklist

☑ Select book for surprise distribution at end of evening

☑ Theme or don't theme night

☑ Create bites menu of choice

☑ Finalize booktini or other cocktail choice

☑ Select wine

☑ Use *GG* 101 lists to make shopping list

☑ Buy required bites and bevies ingredients

☑ Take inventory of all tableware, glasses and serving pieces

☑ Make music selection

☑ Make ice or purchase, if necessary

☑ Borrow supplies, if necessary

☑ Wash and polish all tableware, glassware, etc.

☑ Buy cocktail napkins – an eclectic collection can be fun

☑ Wrap books, if desired

☑ Set table for dining and cocktail area for appetizers

☑ Have taxi numbers handy

☑ Prepare bites and bevies

☑ Turn on music

☑ Adjust lighting, light candles

☑ Open wine

☑ Have books ready for distribution

☑ Greet guests when they arrive

gg discovery

Serve a booktini when your group first arrives, then switch to a your wine choice when serving bites. Also have an assortment of bottled waters and/or juices on hand.

· · · · · · · · · ·

thank you

· ·

There were many times during the writing of this book that we wondered if we had lost our minds. Who did we think we were writing a book? Besides, we're not authors. But we had a genuine desire to share great experiences from our book club meetings and travels with other women. This endeavor would not have been even remotely possible without the ongoing support of our husbands, our best friends: Alex Jongsma, Ken Maaten and Ron Rau. Thank you for your unending patience during our many evening and weekend absences and for your huge faith in our ability to complete the book. A special thank you to Ron for donating his boardroom and office facilities for what turned into a 'camp-out' for a few years.

We resisted the advice to hire professional photographers, photo shoot stylists, and renting studio space to produce our artistic content.

Believing that we could tackle everything on our own , we enlisted the support of two *GG* daughters. Madison D'Andrea (Kathleen's daughter) and Alyssa Jongsma (Perry's daughter) took our photos while we acted as our own stylists. We are so proud of their results; they are truly following in their mothers' footsteps.

To the extent that we wanted to do as much as possible ourselves, there are aspects of publishing a book that simply require professionals. Dave Chilton provided encouragement to us in our early days, and introduced us to our editor Fina Scroppo. Fina provided her expertise in editing and continually kept us focused and on track when it looked like there was no way our initial feeble attempts would ever represent a publishable result. What started as a book concept with a few illustrations and sidebars mushroomed to the polished finished product under the watchful creative eye of Stephanie White, our artistic director. Fina and Stephanie, if it wasn't for your efforts, we never would have been able to deliver the end result. A heartfelt thanks to Dimas De Campos at Andora Graphics for his generosity and patience as he guided us through the complexities of the printing process.

Thank you to our informal focus group, the friends and family that took the time out of their busy schedules to read our early drafts and provide helpful and invaluable feedback. We would also like to thank the entire group of *GG*s, our book club sisters, for their camaraderie and continued support during this very long process. As well to the one *GG* who graciously opened her home to allow her garden and library to be featured in our photo collection.

And last, but certainly not least, we need to thank each other. The bond between *GG*s, for which we want everyone else to celebrate, was truly tested during the writing of this book. It not only survived but also continued to flourish.

perry pat kathleen

Cin-Cin. Relax it's time to play."
—*Cinzano advertisement*